Delivering High Performance

Delivering High Performance

The Third Generation Organisation

DOUGLAS G. LONG

Routledge
Taylor & Francis Group

LONDON AND NEW YORK

First published 2013 by Gower Publishing

Published 2016 by Routledge
2 Park Square, Milton Park, Abingdon, Oxfordshire OX14 4RN
711 Third Avenue, New York, NY 10017, USA

First issued in paperback 2016

Routledge is an imprint of the Taylor & Francis Group, an informa business

Gower Applied Business Research
Our programme provides leaders, practitioners, scholars and researchers with thought
provoking, cutting edge books that combine conceptual insights, interdisciplinary rigour and
practical relevance in key areas of business and management.

British Library Cataloguing in Publication Data
A catalogue record for this book is available from the British Library.

The Library of Congress has cataloged the printed edition as follows:
Long, Douglas G.
 Delivering high performance : the third generation organisation / by Douglas G. Long.
   pages cm
 Includes bibliographical references and index.
 ISBN 978-1-4724-1332-1 (hardback)
1. Organizational effectiveness. 2. Leadership. 3. Organizational
change. 4. Performance. 5. Employee motivation. I. Title.

 HD58.9.L663 2013
 658.4'06--dc23

                                                                    2013010234

ISBN 13: 978-1-138-27957-5 (pbk)
ISBN 13: 978-1-4724-1332-1 (hbk)

Contents

List of Figures and Tables

Figures

Tables

If a company is successful it is due to the efforts of everyone in it, but if it fails it is because of the failure of the board. If the board fails it is the responsibility of the chairman, notwithstanding the collective responsibility of everyone. Despite this collective responsibility, it is on the chairman's shoulders that the competition and the performance of that supreme directing body depends.

Sir John Harvey-Jones, 'The Company Chairman',
as quoted in *Third Generation Leadership and the Locus of Control*

About the Author

The author of *Third Generation Leadership and the Locus of Control: Knowledge, Change and Neuroscience* now provides a 'how to' work that looks at the implementation of Third Generation Leadership principles. The core of the book is the case study of a manufacturing company that grew its revenues from $55 million to $70 million in two years and improved its Earnings Before Interest and Tax (EBIT) from around $1 million to around $11 million in the same period.

Douglas G. Long was born in New Zealand but has lived in Australia for most of his life. His tertiary education was in New Zealand, Australia, England and the United States, culminating in 1985 with a PhD in Organisational Psychology.

For many years he taught in universities in Australia and the United States including David Syme Business School, RMIT Graduate College of Management and Drexel University. From 1988 to 2000 he was associated with Macquarie Graduate School of Management in Sydney where he researched, designed and delivered the programme Leadership in Senior Management. Since 2003 he has held a post as a Casual Academic with Australia's Southern Cross University Graduate College of Management where he supervises candidates studying for their degree of DBA.

Along with this, he has been an active consultant specialising in leadership and change with public and private sector clients throughout Australia, New Zealand and South East Asia. In this role he has facilitated some major changes undergone by very large Australian and South East Asian organisations. He is an accomplished public speaker and public speaking has taken him to conferences in Australia, New Zealand, Singapore, Malaysia, Japan, The Netherlands, Finland, Spain, Brazil and the United States.

He has been involved in community service for most of his life. For 16 years he was a member of the St John Ambulance Brigade and, in Melbourne, after he was appointed a Justice of the Peace, he sat on the Bench at two local Magistrates' Courts for several years. In 1983 he was brought in to coordinate the State Relief Centre operations for the disastrous Ash Wednesday Bush Fires in Victoria.

Douglas now lives in Sydney, Australia, and is married with five children and five grandchildren.

Apart from *Third Generation Leadership and the Locus of Control: Knowledge, Change and Neuroscience* he is the author of five earlier books:

- *Learner Managed Learning: The Key to Lifelong Learning and Development;*

- *Competitive Advantage in the 21st Century: From Vision into Action;*

- *The Challenge of the Diamond;*

- *Leaders: Diamonds or Cubic Zirconia? Asia Pacific Leaders on Leadership;*

- *The Curse of PPM and How to Remove It.*

And a co-author (with Andrew Mowat and John Corrigan) of:

- *The Success Zone: 5 Powerful Steps for Growing Yourself and Leading Others.*

Introduction

We were at the fifth tee, waiting for the group in front to clear the green, when I heard one of my regular golfing partners say to a third member of our group, 'Why don't you speak to Doug about the problem?' I turned and looked at them both – my friend and his guest – and commented that, after my three-putt from two metres on the last green it had better not be about golf. It wasn't. It turned out that this man was co-owner and CEO of a manufacturing company that employed about 350 people (of which about 100 were employed on a casual or short-term contract basis) around Australia. The company had a turnover of around $55 million.[1] Recently the company had plateaued and despite the best efforts of management, costs were going up and profits were decreasing. We agreed to meet during the coming week.

Two years later, with no increase in staff or gearing, revenues had increased by some $15 million and, of this, about $10 million was going to the bottom line. This book tells how the transformation came about and it provides you, the reader, with the same core questions and approaches that were used to bring it about. The book starts with the presentation of the case study that eventually resulted from this discussion on the fifth tee. This case study illustrates how the approaches set out in Chapters 1 through 6 are used to achieve this spectacular result.

In September 2012 Gower Publishing, UK released my book *Third Generation Leadership and the Locus of Control: Knowledge, Change and Neuroscience*. Since then I have received emails and phone calls from all around the world from people who were excited by this different concept. These people were interested in the varying quality of leadership required at differing levels in an organisation and in how a Third Generation Leadership approach actually worked across an entire entity. Invariably one of the questions they asked related to the issue of individual, unit

---

1   All references to dollars in the text are Australian dollars.

and organisational performance. Of particular interest was the issue of 'performance management' or 'performance appraisal' and how these were affected and/or could be implemented by a Third Generation Leadership approach. Questions relating to achieving and maintaining a high-performing organisation were frequently asked.

Around the same time several organisations in Australia and New Zealand approached me regarding management development. These organisations were seeking a programme that would be applicable across a diverse range of work areas and levels of management. They wanted to develop practical people leadership skills in order to achieve high performance and foster high levels of staff engagement.

This book is a response to both sets of these enquiries. However it does not re-examine the concept of Third Generation Leadership; instead it follows on from that book to open a new discussion about the issue of obtaining and maintaining performance when an organisation is using a Third Generation Leadership approach. Starting with a case study that shows what is possible, the book then moves to provide the tools and processes that form the Third Generation Leadership approach.

The book is a combination of 'information' and 'practice'. Every chapter ends with both a chapter summary and a series of practical activities that can be undertaken in order to develop and maintain the level of performance desired. If you like, this is a 'how to' book that gives the reader practical tools that can be immediately applied. However it must be stressed that following this process is not a guarantee that productivity and overall performance will be improved – in any given situation there are too many variables for any such guarantees. But based on more than 25 years' experience across organisations in a wide variety of industries and countries (and as illustrated in the case study), following the process has had a very positive experience on a range of organisations that had revenues initially ranging from around $1 million to $billions. Some examples:

- A small business, turnover $1.17million with a profit of around $100,000 and employing nine people, grew its revenues to $5.3 million and its profits to $1.35 million in four years with staff numbers remaining the same.

- A large business with turnover around $1.3 billion with profits around $180 million and employing 5,000 people – most of whom were members of trade unions, in five years, grew its revenues to $1.6 billion for profits of around $300 million while reducing staffing levels to 3,500 without any industrial disputes or employee unrest.

- An Australian bank tried out a Third Generation Leadership application for ten weeks and assessed the impact. The bank was totally in control of the assessment. They decided to try it out in one area in Sydney. By the bank's own assessment, at the end of the ten weeks:

  - the total new revenue to the bank from this single unit was $7,409,000;
  - new revenue from this single unit annualised was $29,636,000.

This process succeeds because of the way it enhances engagement of people at every level of the organisation and the way in which it creates an environment where there is a significantly improved probability of success being attained.

A word of warning. While every organisation with which I have worked has had very positive experiences with the processes outlined in this book, to date only one – Briysun Corporation – has achieved absolutely spectacular improvement. I make no predictions as to the degree of improvement your organisation can obtain but, based on over 25 years' experience, I do believe that, by following this process, improvement is possible for every organisation.

Finally a word of thanks to my colleague Ian Freeman for suggestions he made after reading an early draft of this book.

Case Study:
A $15 Million Productivity
Increase in Two Years

As said in the Introduction, the processes provided in this book have all been used very successfully as discrete units over a period of some 25 years with large and small organisations across Australia, New Zealand, Indonesia, Singapore, Malaysia, Thailand, Vietnam, Hong Kong, Taiwan and Papua New Guinea. These client organisations encompassed for-profit and not-for-profit operations in government, professional practices, finance, energy organisations, communications, manufacturing, primary industry and general service businesses. The size of these organisations when I started working with them ranged from one with revenues of just over $1 million and comprising only nine people in one location, to organisations with revenues in the billions and comprising thousands of people spread across several continents. However it was not until after a discussion that commenced on the fifth tee of a golf course that the opportunity arose to link together all of these processes.

The following case study is the story of how bringing all of these processes together created a comprehensive approach that produced spectacular results for one specific organisation. Prior to embarking on this Third Generation Leadership approach, the organisation involved had been considering closing its manufacturing operations in Australia and, like so many other businesses, moving this work off-shore. In the first three-year period of implementing this new process the results achieved in this organisation (Briysun Corporation) are vastly better than I have seen in any other organisation with which I have worked.

In some respects, this case study is an anomaly because Briysun's is the first to use the complete Third Generation Leadership approach. However, based on earlier experience with the various components of the process, it is my firm belief that any organisation can obtain significant benefits by following the complete process outlined in this book. The Briysun Corporation case study then becomes an illustration of what is possible. This case study is a graphic example of what can happen when you involve everyone in a change process and it clearly illustrates the message made by a *Harvard Business Review* Blog[1] in December 2012 that stressed the need for ensuring that important changes actually reach and involve the most remote stakeholders, whether they are front-line workers or customers.

At the time of publication the company involved has not completed its first five-year 'dream with a date' cycle and so, for commercial reasons, all identifying features (including the name Briysun Corporation) have been changed at their request.

Briysun Corporation

BACKGROUND

We were at the fifth tee, waiting for the group in front to clear the green of this 183 metre par 3, when I heard one of my regular golfing partners say to a third member of our group, 'Why don't you speak to Doug about the problem?' I turned and looked at them both – my friend and his guest – and commented that, after my three-putt from two metres on the last green it had better not be about golf. It wasn't. It turned out that this man, Harry, was co-owner and CEO of a manufacturing, distribution and servicing company that employed about 350 people (of which slightly more than 100 were employed on a casual basis) mainly around Australia and New Zealand. The company had a turnover of around $55 million. Over recent years the company had plateaued and despite the best efforts of management, costs were going up and profits were decreasing.

Harry told me that, following the completion of his apprenticeship, he had stayed with his then employer (a small owner-operated business) for six years before the ill-health of his employer meant that the business faced closure. He and a fellow tradesman, Brian, believed that the business had potential and they were able to negotiate a buy-out with payment to be made over several

---

1   December 2012, http://blogs.hbr.org/ashkenas/2012/12/in-a-change-effort-start-with.html? utm_source=feedburner&utm_medium=feed&utm_campaign=Feed%3A+harvardbusiness+% 28HBR.org%29&utm_content=Google+Reader&goback=.gde_63688_member_195048969.

years. 20 years ago that buy-out was completed and Briysun had grown over the succeeding years. It now employed some 350 people across Australia with the majority of these at its factory in a well-known industrial location and its revenues had grown from around $7 million when they initiated the buy-out to its current level. They had small sales and services teams in each capital city but, although they had some export sales (mainly to New Zealand) they saw no need to have more offices. Harry and Brian still ran the company and, through their family trusts, were its sole shareholders. Reflecting Harry and Brian's roots as apprentices and tradesmen, the company was fully unionised even though union membership was voluntary. We agreed to meet during the coming week.

THE INITIAL BRIEFING

At our meeting later that week, I met Brian and found that the two were very similar – straight forward tradesmen whose business education had come from 'the school of hard knocks'. They had always recognised their limitations and so had surrounded themselves with good, well-qualified professionals in all management and financial areas. Over the years things had become increasingly competitive mainly from the introduction of overseas-owned operations increasing their inroads to the Australian market. Most (if not all) of these new competitors did virtually all of their manufacturing in Asian countries that had far lower wages and associated costs than did Australia. This competition had resulted in decreased profits and where once the business had provided secure employment to its people and a good return to its owners, Earnings Before Interest and Tax (EBIT) had been dropping and, for the last financial year, was below $1 million despite an aggressive cost reduction programme. Fortunately they had a very low gearing so, right now, they could survive but the question was, 'For how long?' They were considering closing the local operations and moving their manufacturing base off-shore.

Both Harry and Brian wanted to maintain their Australian manufacturing base. Although they knew that moving manufacturing off-shore was a feasible option (and one recommended by their auditors and bankers as well as by other professional advisors) they had a moral dilemma about this. They were concerned that Australia was losing much of its manufacturing industry and they saw how this was impacting on employment and how it was having a negative social impact in many areas. They knew that if they moved their operations off-shore this would seriously affect families – many of which they considered friends – in their local community. However such a move had to be now under serious consideration as they pondered their survival. While not yet at a crisis point, the warning signs of an impending disaster were increasingly apparent and action would need to be taken very soon.

I talked about the Adizes life cycle assessment and, after briefly explaining it, I asked Harry, Brian and the three executives to nominate where they thought Briysun was. Harry and Brian both had the company rated at 'the fall' because they felt the company was losing the drive and vibrancy it once had but the others had the company around the 'founders' trap' because they felt that the limitations placed upon the company – such as keeping manufacturing in Australia – were holding the company back. These differences of opinion led to some very frank and open discussions in which everyone's existing views were seriously challenged. I then suggested that both Harry and Brian, together with their executives, independently complete the Adizes life cycle assessment and that we should meet in a week for everyone to share the data from this so that, then, we could consider the way forward. This was agreed and, over the next week, the Adizes assessment was duly completed by five people including Harry and Brian. (Please see Figure 2.2 on page 53 for a diagram of the Adizes life cyle.)

When we next met and shared the data the results surprised everyone – there was general agreement that Briysun was either 'stable' but heading towards 'aristocracy' or at 'adolescence' and facing 'premature ageing'. In the ensuing discussion it then quickly became apparent that, although Harry and Brian prided themselves on having an 'open' management style in which people were encouraged to speak their minds, such discussions when they did take place, had always been on a one-with-one basis and, until only a week previous (at the first meeting with me), the entire executive team had never aired them in their group meetings. By the end of the discussion it was agreed that Briysun should be in 'prime' and it was also agreed that we would go for a two-day retreat to determine both what 'prime' would look like and how to get there.

COMMENCING THE THIRD GENERATION LEADERSHIP APPROACH

A couple of weeks later we were at a conference centre and I introduced the Vision into Action process. At the end of the two days it had been agreed:

> **Vision** To be an Australian manufacturing success story that is renowned for our community awareness and social concern while providing secure long-term employment for our people along with a return to our owners that is better than they could obtain from any other investment.

Mission To be a manufacturing operation that sells and services its own products in all markets where it operates.

Values We are an Australian business that will keep its manufacturing operations in Australia.

We care for our people no matter what their role in the company and this means we will, at all times, treat them with respect; be totally honest in our dealings with each and every person; and will remunerate everyone in a manner that our people agree is fair and equitable.

We are a customer-focused organisation which means that we will maintain a positive relationship with all customers and prospective customers; we will not promise what we cannot deliver; we will be transparent in our pricing and accommodating but firm in our revenue collection; and, in cases where we are not able to supply what is sought, we will recommend appropriate alternative suppliers who may be able to meet the customer's needs.

We have a strong social conscience which means that we will support local sporting teams, service clubs and charities where possible and that we will have a regular intake of local young people as apprentices and trainees even though we recognise that, in many cases, the training we supply may eventually be of most benefit to other organisations.

Dream with a Date By the end of 2014 we will have revenues approaching $80 million and an EBIT of around 20 per cent. Our gearing will be similar to that of today and we will still employ around 350 people based around our Australian manufacturing plant.

Immediately following the executive retreat, Harry and Brian brought all 350 personnel to the head office for a day (paying for overnight accommodation and all other expenses where necessary) and shared their desire to remain an Australian manufacturing operation as well as their broad plans for growth. They then briefly explained the Third Generation Leadership process and how it would involve everyone in developing and implementing the way forward. At this meeting, emphasis was placed on sharing and explaining the values that had been agreed and obtaining feedback as to how the employees felt about these.

Briysun had three divisions – manufacturing and service, finance and administration, and marketing and sales. There was one executive responsible for each of these areas and each of these executives then took his or her direct reports to a one-day retreat where they started with the dream with a date then determined what this meant in terms of objectives and strategies as well as considering any 'ouch points' that existed or could exist with the key players and the organisational culture. Each area developed approaches ideally to prevent, but also to deal with, all recognised 'ouch points'. Implementing the cascading manager-once-removed approach, either Harry or Brian was present throughout each of these sessions.

Where appropriate because of organisational levels, this process was then repeated for the next levels of supervision with an executive (or other 'manager once removed') being present to support the person who was conducting the retreat. The result was that within a month of the executive retreat, everyone in the company (including all casual employees) had been involved in a workshop to help them understand what was happening and at which they were encouraged to provide feedback and suggestions that could be used in the implementation phase. After every such workshop, a summary of the process and outputs was prepared and distributed to every person who was involved at that level as well as a copy being passed 'up the line'. This promoted an iterative process of planning.

INITIAL REACTIONS

Despite Harry and Brian being well known and liked by most of the employees, there was a lot of suspicion and disbelief at this stage of the process. Most of the older employees (aged over 30) had worked in at least one other organisation during their working life and, from experience, many of these people had an ingrained mistrust of 'management' even when 'management' came from a background very similar to their own. It quickly became clear that Briysun had to address its culture and a key part of this was recognised as being a change in executive and management behaviour. There was considerable discussion at this point because both Harry and Brian were used to fast action and quick results and it was not easy for them to accept that bringing about the changes that Briysun's needed was going to be a long (at least three to four years) and relatively expensive process. In order to deal with this concern about time and costs it was agreed that the project would be broken down into a series of milestones with re-evaluation of the process and some form of cost–benefit analysis being done when each milestone was reached.

Both Harry and Brian later commented that this stage of deciding to engage in the total Third Generation Leadership process – which started with a detailed research and diagnosis phase – really tested their commitment to having both a short-term and a long-term focus for Briysun because they were not used to (or comfortable with) waiting for results.

THE FIRST YEAR

For many years Briysun had been using one of the situational approaches for the training of supervisors and managers. Because this was known and accepted it was decided to continue with this approach but to see whether its implementation could be improved. Focus groups were held and these involved everyone who had undergone Briysun's leadership and/or management training. The question discussed in each focus group related to problems in implementing what they had learned and ways of addressing these problems. At these sessions it became clear that there was little real support currently given to supervisors and/or managers during and immediately after any training programme and that, as a result, intentions of behaviour change seldom became reality. A constant comment related to the pressures involved in needing to continue actively doing one's everyday work simultaneously with participating in any training. This meant that each participant's attention was constantly split between dealing with 'back at work' issues through phone calls, emails and so on and participating in the course. Three things were agreed from this input. First, it was decided to provide Briysun's leadership training to every employee (including all casuals) so that the approach to be expected from supervisors and managers was widely known. Second, it was agreed that a new approach would be introduced around training – an approach in which trainees should become largely free from workplace concerns while undergoing training. And third it was decided to develop and implement a mentoring and cognitive coaching programme. A key part of this mentoring and cognitive coaching programme was the 'red zone–blue zone' dichotomy of Third Generation Leadership and the importance of shifting one's brain's locus of control into the blue zone.

The first two steps were immediately implemented and by the end of the first year the mentoring and cognitive coaching programme was also fully operational. Also at this first review stage it became clear that even after a period as short as one year there was a different, far more positive culture evolving at Briysun. The evidence of this was the volume and quality of suggestions that, partly because of the on-going mapping and flow charting process, were now initiating at factory floor level and which, in almost every case, resulted in better work practices and higher productivity in the factory. These suggestions also had brought about improved cash flow control and increased sales through staff-initiated innovative marketing and sales approaches.

Also towards the end of the first year it was decided to totally redesign the performance appraisal system. The starting point for this was to bring a group of suppliers and non-competing customers into a Briysun workshop for a half day and ask them to describe their 'ideal' Briysun. All suggestions were recorded and, out of these, a questionnaire was developed to be taken to as many customers and suppliers as possible. When the questionnaire had been developed, every person at Briysun who had any customer or supplier contact (including all executives) was required to be involved in an action research process by visiting at least three customers with the questionnaire which recorded both a rating for each item (one through five, with five being exemplary) and an explanation of why that rating was given. This exercise was undertaken in pairs with each pair comprising a person from different divisions and it was completed in two months. This process was followed for both Australian and international customers and suppliers. All up, around 150 people across all divisions were involved. Each pair went through a debriefing on return from each customer/supplier interview and, when all interviews were completed, focus groups were held in which the interviewers discussed the responses they had received; their feelings about these responses; and suggestions were made as to how things could be improved.

This exercise did three critical things. First it meant that people who had only known customers or suppliers through telephone, email or letter actually met some of these people face-to-face and so they became aware of them as a 'person' rather than simply as a name or a number. Second it enabled everyone to understand where the company was falling down on customer orientation and how this could be addressed. The third effect was that barriers between divisions were broken down so that manufacturing and service, finance and administration, and marketing and sales people came to understand some of the problems and issues that existed across divisions. People at all levels were then encouraged to work together across divisions to overcome or eliminate these problems or issues.

THE SECOND YEAR

Based initially on the information obtained from this exercise, a 'bottom-up' performance appraisal process was then developed and an on-going customer satisfaction survey process (using a very similar format) was introduced that, on an on-going basis, would mean every person (from Harry and Brian down) with any form of customer or supplier contact would visit at least two customers every year.

By half-way through the second year it was apparent that Briysun was well on the way to recreating itself. The evidence for this was the very high level of engagement and almost total commitment that now existed throughout the organisation. This high level of engagement and almost total commitment had come about because of the new way in which Harry, Brian and the executive exercised their leadership. The atmosphere was now developing to one of trust in which productivity improvement suggestions were continually being made and this had resulted in several large-step improvements. Both Harry and Brian and their executives frequently commented that in their earlier cost-cutting approaches they would never have considered some of the options suggested from the lower-level employees. The atmosphere throughout the organisation was increasingly collaborative with creativity and innovation being seen everywhere. It was very apparent that, once the right environment had been created by the executive, the quality of immediate leadership provided throughout the organisation was *the* critical factor in significantly improving productivity.

Primarily because of suggestions made at the grass roots level of Briysun, by the end of the second year, with no increase in staff or gearing, revenues had increased by some $15 million and, of this, about $10 million were EBIT. This result was brought about by increased productivity right across Briysun coupled with higher sales revenues and reduced supplier costs negotiated by changing payment and delivery terms. Although staffing numbers overall had remained the same, suggestions relating to productivity improvement meant that about half those who had initially been employed on a casual basis were now employed on a permanent basis. Harry and Brian fully recognised that improvements of this magnitude were highly unlikely in the future as the major productivity gains had now been made but it was clear that the dream with a date had a high probability of being realised through the on-going incremental improvements that were still possible.

MOVING FORWARD

It is now almost to the end of the third year of this process and the executive are preparing to head away to a second two-day retreat to review progress to date and to repeat the Vision into Action process with a dream with a date that will focus on the end of 2020.

A RETROSPECTIVE

In looking back over these three years, both Harry and Brian say that, from a personal perspective, the hardest parts have been first, moving away from any form of a 'command and control' type of management and second, the sharing of certain information.

In relation to moving away from 'command and control', neither Brian nor Harry was ever particularly authoritarian in their management style but both admit that there were times when they demanded things be done in a certain way or at a certain time because, in their eyes, this was the best way or time for such activities to occur. In retrospect they now realise that their controlling approach actually prevented the company from making many of the productivity improvements that have helped transform the operations.

In relation to sharing of certain information, Harry and Brian also admit that it has been hard releasing some things that traditionally they had kept 'close to their chests' because these impacted on matters affecting their family trusts – only the company secretary and the auditors had been privy to certain details. Now the sharing of much more of this information is enabling all their executives to better understand some decision-making processes. This has proved very positive in terms of enhancing a team concept at the top of the organisation.

MAPPING AND FLOW CHARTING

When asked about the difficulties experienced in the change process, both Harry and Brian rated the initial research and the mapping of all the organisation's processes as being the most tedious and time-consuming parts. The development of an organisation-wide process map and detailed flow charts for every part of the organisation's operations from the ordering of materials through to the banking of revenues meant that every employee was involved to some extent and, because of the time involved, there was a need to employ additional temporary staff at times. As Harry and Brian euphemistically put it:

> There were some interesting, heated, and detailed 'creative discussions' among the executive and with the consultant over this period as we could see money being spent without any obvious benefit – we understood what was being done and why it was being done but a lot of this was being done out of faith and trust in the consultant rather than because we really believed it was necessary. Now we're pleased that we stuck with it because this really enabled us to see where duplication occurred and where bottle necks existed – we realise now that earlier we had often been dealing with symptoms rather than causes. With this information we could explore new approaches and that accounts for a lot of the huge improvements we experienced in year two. The other thing about this is that by now ensuring we are keeping the flow charts up to date at all times, we are making sure we are always monitoring for further improvements.

They point out that the flow charts are maintained by the people who actually do the work so that any changes are immediately logged and results recorded.

CUSTOMERS AND SUPPLIERS

When asked about the most surprising thing that had happened over the past three years, both Harry and Brian talked about their experience with customers and suppliers. Although they had always known that price was important, Brian and Harry had always stressed that their sales should never be based primarily on price – they argued that selling primarily on price was a good way to eventually go broke because once customers realised that this was happening, there would be continual pressure on margins until the business lost viability. Despite this the meetings with the customers had ascertained that some of their sales team had slipped into this 'selling on price' trap. The information obtained from the interview contact with customers then proved to be a very effective tool for moving away from any 'selling on price' approach – in part because it was now recognised that failure to remedy the 'selling on price' approach could hasten any move to close the Australian manufacturing operations.

Harry and Brian stated they were both amazed at the positive response they got from external customers and suppliers regarding this interview phase.

First, when they approached customers and suppliers about joining a focus group to ascertain 'the ideal Briysun', they found not only were people keen to participate but also that most of them stated they would be quite happy to have their competitors in the same focus group. While the first of these was anticipated by Harry and Brian, the situation with competitor customers was not. Second, when Briysun staff came to visit customers and suppliers and used the questionnaire that had been developed there was unequivocal praise for the survey. As a consequence, customers and suppliers readily volunteered additional information that was of benefit to Briysun.

Key actions that arose from the customer and supplier surveys and interviews were that:

- in some cases, suppliers suggested they could be even more competitive in their pricing if Briysun was able to use different delivery and/or creditor payment terms;

- a number of customers agreed that they would be willing to pay a premium for Briysun's products if those products could meet different delivery and payment arrangements.

Both of these actions were very instrumental in simultaneously increasing revenues and either holding or reducing costs – a major benefit to Briysun's bottom line without any detrimental impact on third parties.

- Some of the other suggestions made at these interview surveys also enabled Briysun to significantly increase its export market.

WHAT THE EMPLOYEES THINK

Harry and Brian suggested that people across the organisation should be spoken with in order to ascertain employee response to the changes that had taken place and the new Briysun that was emerging. They placed no restrictions on who could be spoken with nor requested any report back from the meetings. The interviews with employees proved a valuable and interesting exercise.

Briysun's staff was a real cross-section of Australian citizens. People of almost every race, language, colour and creed were employed and although English was the lingua franca of the company it was not unusual to hear a wide range of languages at any break or down time because, for many, English was a second or third language and, for some, there was quite a low level of English language competency. While some of the employees were university educated and others had trade or similar qualifications, there were many people who had received little or no formal education and one or two of the people were close to illiterate. A few employees had served prison or other custodial or non-custodial sentences for various offences. Many of the employees had been with the company for quite a long time and about five had been there almost as long as Harry and Brian had been in charge.

There was no argument from any of the people interviewed about the fact that Briysun was a different company now from what it had been a few years before. They all said it seemed to be more people friendly than in the past and they all agreed that it was now a busier and more interesting place at which to work. It was also interesting to note that they all could describe most of Briysun's vision and they all commented favourably on the new value set. There were very positive comments made about the information and training they had received about leadership. Whether or not people had any formal leadership responsibility as a leading hand, foreman, supervisor or manager, it was widely commented that everyone had benefited by understanding the leadership training that was given to those with supervisory or management responsibility. People said that this helped them see what was trying to be done as well as to understand more of the pressures that their immediate leaders experienced. They also said that by making sure everyone was familiar with the company's leadership model there was a far greater probability that the training would be implemented – any behavioural lapses could be seen and were commented upon. Everyone said that it was now the best place at which they had ever worked. These were the positives.

On the not so positive side it was clear that there was still some degree of scepticism as to the permanence of the changes. People were quick to regale anecdotes about when Harry, Brian or one of the executives or someone else in a management or supervisory role reverted to their old way of interacting – and there were a lot of these anecdotes because, even with the best intentions in the world, supervisors and managers found it easy to lapse into their previous behaviour patterns. (Although it was noted that these lapses were becoming less frequent.) Many of the older employees commented that their past experience included working with organisations that claimed to be changing yet, when things went awry, they found that the company reverted to its previous pattern – most of those in the factory had been retrenched from previous positions at least once over the years. A number of these made comments along the lines of 'right now things are going well – we've more work than ever before, there's a lot less complaints from customers, and workplace safety is better than its ever been; but what will happen when things get tight? Will Harry and Brian then continue this approach of sharing information and asking for suggestions from everybody as to how things can be improved? Don't get us wrong, we love what has happened and this is an even better place to work than it's ever been, but we'll just have to wait and see what happens down the track.' It was clear that people wanted to believe that the changes and improvements were permanent but they were also very aware of the fact that, in reality, it is very seldom that there are any guarantees in the work place.

QUO VADIS?

This is an on-going story. Harry and Brian have committed to the process continuing for at least another five years as they believe they still need support rather than standing totally on their own. They believe that Briysun Corporation is now well on its way to achieving their 2014 dream with a date and, according to Harry and Brian, the fees they have incurred are minor in comparison with the returns they have achieved. In accord with the suggestions made by Colin Price and Scott Keller (see Chapter 2) – although totally unaware of Price and Keller's work when Brisyun started its journey in 2010 – they have found a different, far more effective way of achieving superior performance (although its not Price's 'plate spinning'!). Briysun is now well on the way to being a high-performing organisation.

1

Overview – Understanding the Full Performance Conundrum

Third Generation Leadership is all about a different way of achieving results. A high-performing organisation is one that is recognised for obtaining on-going desired performance through a highly productive work force. In other words, high levels of productivity and performance are the key indicators of a high-performing organisation.

One of the concerns I have about many management and political commentators is that, too often, we are regaled with 'either/or' type approaches that label people or approaches as being 'left wing' or 'right wing' (or something in between) and it is quite common to find advocates of any economic approach being influenced (either overtly or covertly) by their personal political orientation. We see this 'either/or' situation in every case where a writer or commentator denigrates any view that is counter to his or her own. Far too often this then degenerates into what is close to a simplistic approach of how we can fix the world's ills through some form of either a modern socialism or modern capitalism that invariably focuses on relatively short-term time frames and which fails to deal with the increasing levels of ambiguity and complexity that are part and parcel of everyday life in this twenty-first century.

There is a recent example of this sort of writing in the UK newspaper, *The Telegraph*,[1] when one of their writers, Janet Daley, accuses both the UK and the US as being complicit in 'signing their own death warrant' because of the dispute, in the US, regarding avoiding the 'fiscal cliff' and, in the UK, because of a failure to cut back on areas of social welfare including the UK's National Health Service. She makes a very strong case for her position which, obviously, is very supportive of a strong capitalist view and she rightly points out that

---

1 http://www.telegraph.co.uk/news/politics/georgeosborne/9730434/The-West-is-signing-its-own-death-sentence.html, December 8, 2012.

capitalism is dynamic and, by its very nature, does create inequalities of wealth. However the main thrust of her contention is that this dynamism means a strongly capitalistic society must be maintained as, in her view, this is the only way for economic survival. She argues that we are witnessing the 'collapse of the most successful economic experiment in human history' as though relatively recent successes (and the US-dominated version of capitalism has been extremely successful over the past 75 or so years) is the ultimate pinnacle of economic evolution. In that regard she is not totally dissimilar (although from a diametrically opposite perspective) to Karl Marx who argued that his version of communism would be the ultimate peak of economic evolution – and we all know that his approach was never proven to be an outstanding economic success and we all know how that experiment finished! Daley at least has historical evidence on her side and, unlike Marx who was arguing from a theoretical perspective, she has the strength of arguing from established fact. Of course there are writers just as strong on the other side (for example Jeffrey Sachs – see Chapter 6) who also argue that the current emphasis is failing but that rediscovering a moral base that contains elements of socialism – but not communistic – is the only way for economic survival.

Despite Janet Daley's powerful and impassioned plea, the truth is that experience shows neither socialism or capitalism work when taken to extremes – the fall of the USSR some 20 years ago and the current economic woes of the US and in the European Economic Community (EEC) can both be seen as evidence of this. (Although those who are strongly capitalistic would claim that the failure in the EEC was caused by some form of creeping socialism rather than by the excesses of capitalism that brought about the Global Financial Crisis that started in 2007.)

Many years ago I suggested that we were moving to a new economic reality where we would be no longer living in either a capitalistic or a socialistic age.[2] I argued that in this new age we needed to take a different approach to obtaining results – an approach in which economic success was critical but, which had its emphasis on both individual and collective economic success; which focused on working *with* people so that they were both engaged and committed in their work. This approach necessitates that the leadership of any and every organisation that seeks a highly productive work force must have (or be capable of developing) the skills to deal with increasingly large amounts of complexity and ambiguity. Such an approach requires that we manage

---

2   Long, Douglas G., 'Personnel Management in the Post Capitalistic Age', *Asia Pacific Journal of Human Resources*, Vol 22, No. 4, November 1984.

(or lead) people in a different manner from what has been the case in the past. It requires, also, that we recognise the practice of leadership is different at various levels of an organisation – for example, as will be made clear in Chapter 6, board leadership is qualitatively different from executive leadership which, in turn, is different from managerial leadership – and until this is understood there is only a low probability of developing a high-performing organisation.

In all organisations, including nations, performance is the 'bottom line'. High-performing organisations are those that can obtain this performance at a high level over protracted periods of time. But in this early twenty-first century, increasingly we are finding that the 'tried and true' ways of obtaining this desired performance are proving inadequate to the task. The result is that we see economic and social disenchantment leading to significant levels of unrest and political agitation against nations and corporations across the world in both the 'east' and the 'west'. Unfortunately, all too often in national or political situations, the response from authorities is the attempted repression of dissent – and frequently this repression is exhibited in violent action causing death and destruction on both sides. In all these cases there are really no winners.

There has to be a better way.

I suggest that Third Generation Leadership provides some insight into a potentially better way – a possible way forward. Third Generation Leadership focuses on performance and looks at the role of leadership in bringing about this performance through commitment of those responsible for delivering what is sought. This new approach is neither 'capitalist' nor 'socialist' – it is simply a different way of leading at every level and in every area of an organisation – a way that facilitates engagement, personal accountability and high productivity. As I have said, these of course are the hall marks of a high-performing organisation.

However a Third Generation Leadership approach will threaten the status quo in relation to how organisations exercise leadership. That today's approach tends to be confrontational with all the power residing in management is graphically illustrated by a 2012 report in *The Sydney Morning Herald*[3] where people at the grass roots ('labour' as they are referred to in an almost derogatory manner) are told they may not sit down during working hours 'unless their duties demand it'! Clearly the project involved is experiencing significant

---

3   http://www.smh.com.au/opinion/political-news/shorten-questions-if-standing-order-was-written-sitting-down-20121211-2b6to.html, December 11, 2012.

cost over runs but, as high-performing organisations know, high productivity seldom comes as the result of management fiat. Working with people – good leadership – is far more likely to achieve desired goals than is confrontation.

Fortunately examination of the role of leadership is receiving attention in a new way today. In the past the focus on leadership has often been quite narrow and sometimes focused almost exclusively on the attitudes and behaviours of leaders. Today we are finding that through a focus on the *effects* of leadership – the productivity of people and organisations – our understanding of leadership is evolving in a different form.

Recently (July 2012) Edward Lazear and Kathryn Shaw from Stanford University and Christopher Stanton from the University of Utah published a paper titled 'The Value of Bosses'.[4] Covering a period of four years (June 2006 to May 2010), Lazear, Shaw and Stanton were involved in studying the effect of 'the boss' in one very large service company. A total of 23,878 workers and 1,940 bosses (over a total of about 5.7 million worker days) were involved in the study and because of the nature of the work done and the records kept by the company with respect to general customer transactions it was possible to accurately gauge the impact of immediate leaders ('the boss') on productivity.

This research by Lazear, Shaw and Stanton indicated that the quality of immediate leadership provided has a very significant impact on productivity – in fact they argue that an immediate leader who is in the top 10 per cent of leadership quality increases a work group's output by the approximate equivalent of adding one more person to a nine-member group – clearly a good 'boss' or leader has a very significant positive impact on productivity. They found that a boss in the top 10 per cent can increase a person's output by 1.3 units per hour more than is the case with a boss in the lowest 10 per cent. In their research bosses averaged about nine direct reports and each of these people produced about 10.3 units per hour under normal conditions. This means that a good leader could add about 11.7 units per hour which is significantly more than would be obtained by adding an extra physical person. In other words, a good immediate leader can have a major impact on both work area productivity and overall organisational performance – something that, as indicated in the Case Study, became very obvious at Briysun.

For many years, of course, the matter of good leadership has been an on-going subject of research across the world. *McKinsey's*, in October 2012,

---

4 http://www.iza.org/conference_files/Leadership_2012/stanton_c7876.pdf, July 2012.

published a study by Professor Michael Useem[5] of Wharton School, University of Pennsylvania. In this article Useem drew attention to the fact that, over a long time, the fundamentals of leadership – having a vision and a strategy to go with it and being able to communicate effectively and to make good strategic decisions – haven't changed. Researchers and writers may discuss various ways of preparing visions and strategies; various ways of communicating effectively; and a range of approaches to effective strategic decision making – but they all agree that these elements or functions are vital. Useem makes the point that these all need to come together in a coherent fashion 'for any role where you're helping people to get to a more promised land'.

For me, the key phrase here is 'helping people to get to a more promised land' because this focuses attention on the issue of performance – leadership is about helping people move from where they are now to some better place. To do this it is vital that a leader has a vision, a strategy and is both a decision maker and a good communicator.

In *Third Generation Leadership and the Locus of Control: Knowledge, Change and Neuroscience* I introduce the Leadership for Performance model (Figure 1.1) to illustrate the complexity with which any leader or manager must deal if they are seriously interested in achieving performance targets.

The key things about this model are first, that I use the term 'leadership' as an inclusive term that makes no distinction between 'manager' and 'leader'. The second key thing is that it shows the issue of obtaining desired performance targets from any person or organisation is vastly more complicated than simply the commitment and capability of the person or people involved. You can have the most committed and capable people in the world working for you yet still miss performance targets if there are issues in any of the other factors impacting on performance. Third, of course, it becomes imperative to ensure that there is a positive link between 'performance' and 'productivity' because a high-performing organisation must be one in which there are high levels of productivity at all levels. 'Productivity' accordingly means obtaining increased performance or better results through improved utilisation of all existing assets.

The challenge now becomes one of understanding and learning how to apply world best standards in setting performance criteria and implementing the process that has the highest probability of delivering these. As we shall see,

---

5   http://www.mckinsey.com/features/leading_in_the_21st_century/michael_useem, October 2012.

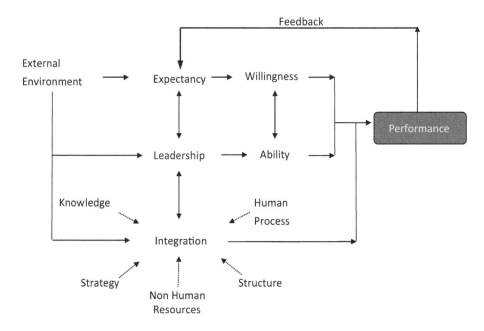

Figure 1.1   **The Leadership for Performance model**

the emphasis must be on 'performance' and the starting point for 'performance' is having a vision into which people can buy and the attainment of which is something to which they can become committed. Unless a leader has the ability to deal with increasing amounts of complexity and can find depths of resilience that perhaps he or she never really knew they had, then he or she will have serious problems – the probability of achieving desired performance will be low.

These are the issues with which we will be grappling.

To understand this Leadership for Performance model, we need to return to *Third Generation Leadership and the Locus of Control*.[6] In that book I wrote:

> *Those factors which directly impact on performance are the 'ability' and 'willingness' or 'readiness' (or, if you prefer, the 'competence' and 'confidence/motivation' or the 'capability') of the individual or group involved. It is important to note that these two factors of ability and willingness are related but totally independent. There are many people*

6   Long, Douglas G., *Third Generation Leadership and the Locus of Control: Knowledge, Change and Neuroscience*, Gower Publishing, Farnham, 2012.

who are competent to do certain things – they have the ability – but they are not prepared to do them: they lack the willingness, confidence or motivation to do them – for some reason or another they lack the 'readiness' to perform. Again, this is not necessarily good or bad – for example all of us have the ability to do things that are unlawful: fortunately most of us are not motivated in that direction and so we can lead relatively quiet, law-abiding lives. On the other hand there are many people who will enthusiastically declare themselves willing to undertake any task even when they have no idea of how the task should be done or what the task involves. Such enthusiasm without skill has either the potential to be very good as some innate competence comes to the fore and they learn quickly or the potential for disaster if what they do proves to endanger themselves and/or other people. It is well known that the effective leader does not confuse willingness with ability.

An important aspect here is the direct relationship between ability and willingness. Generally (but not always) the more capable a person is – the greater their ability – the more likely they are to be willing to demonstrate this ability. Similarly, even if a person has very little ability for a particular task or activity, if they are willing or motivated to learn, there is a high probability that they can develop the requisite ability in a relatively short time. Of course, the reverse is also true. People who have been 'turned off' from education or learning or who are frustrated in their work environment are far less willing to develop new abilities or to demonstrate the abilities they already have.

It is this area that is the focus of most leadership approaches and leadership development programmes. The emphasis of many programmes is on the immediate leader–follower interaction and how the leader encourages a person (or people) towards achieving what needs to be done. There can be no doubt that these factors are crucial to performance and that they warrant the considerable attention they have received. This is a totally appropriate focus for one-on-one or one-on-small-group interactions in environments of low complexity. But the issue of 'willingness' and 'ability' is not sufficient in the majority of situations such as when a larger group is involved or where the leadership is being exercised in more complex situation. For these we need a more inclusive model.

The additional factors that impact less directly on performance are found in two areas – those in the organisation and those in the more distant area of the environment in which the organisation operates ... I will consider first those factors within the organisation – knowledge, strategy, non-human resources, structure and human process – that impact on performance.

'Knowledge' *refers to the aggregation of data and information available – it includes the history of the organisation in a micro and macro sense as well as all the information that is necessary for the organisation to function effectively. Accordingly an essential part of the knowledge component is a high-quality induction programme that links every aspect of every position with the vision, values and strategic orientation of the organisation. But this must be complemented with additional information.*

Traditionally the organisational elders – the leadership team – have been the guardians of this additional knowledge and the ability to impart or withhold information has given these more senior people a significant power base – a power base that is often abused. ...

'Strategy' *refers to the long-term approaches that are in place to help us achieve goals. It takes into account such things as our visions of the future and the goals that we set in order to get there. In commercial organisations (whether for-profit or not-for-profit) the issue of strategy is well known and usually well documented (even if 'strategy' is often confused with 'tactics') but in small organisations and families there may have been no real discussion or planning in this regard, which can lead to 'policy on the run' and decisions being made that are immediately convenient yet which create longer-term problems. It has been said that many of today's problems arise from yesterday's solutions!*

'Non-human resources' *refer to the assets we have available in both the short term and longer term. These may include things like time, cash flow (in a family, monthly wages), buildings, vehicles, machinery and the like. The availability of these for the right people, at the right time, in the right place and for the right use has a very real impact on whether or not people are able to perform as required.*

'**Structure**' *refers to who does what and where everyone fits into the overall need to get things done. This is the aspect that draws together information, strategy and non-human resources. As has often been stated, 'structure should follow strategy' for effective operations. A key aspect of designing the structure relates to ensuring the non-human resources are available when and where required by those who need them. But it also deals with critical people issues such as discrimination. For most of our history there were clear-cut delineations between 'man's work' and 'woman's work', between 'young person's work' and 'old person's work', etc., and such delineations have led etc. in original to many of the stereotypes and discrimination problems we still encounter today.*

It must be noted that, in most organisations, there are two quite distinct structures – the formal one to which assent is given by everyone involved and the informal one which is the network of personal interactions and power alliances that has very significant influence over whether (and how) desired goals are achieved. Both of these structures are important and attention is needed to both if desired performance is to be obtained ... Structure should fit strategy – and sometimes that might mean that neither the existing formal nor the informal structures are appropriate.

'**Human process**' *refers to recruitment, development and the way in which people interact with each other. If the structure is appropriate then this sets up an organisation in which good, highly productive interpersonal relationships are far more likely to exist – of course, the opposite is also true. All people interactions are impacted by the value sets, attitudes, degrees of commitment, willingness to cooperate, and other 'behind the eyes' factors that affect how we behave. The human process factor is not only a key source of high productivity but it is also an area of potential conflict and can be the source of much that makes an organisation dysfunctional. ...*

Each of these factors (knowledge, strategy, non-human resources, structure and human process) on its own has a significant impact on whether or not desired performance is attained. Together they have a multiplier impact on whether or not desired performance is attained. Accordingly it is critical that they are adequately integrated so as to ensure compatibility and harmony. It is the extent to which these factors are appropriately integrated that determines whether or not an organisation has a positive or less than positive organisational culture.

Failure to adequately integrate these factors may well mean that no matter how willing and able a person or group is, they are unable to achieve desired performance because the system is working against them – the culture of the organisation is non-supportive. Leaders who have relatively low conceptual ability generally don't understand this. Invariably such leaders have difficulty in bringing about the appropriate degree of integration and, accordingly, changing the organisation's culture to one that has a high probability of achieving desired results through a committed and engaged workforce. ...

But apart from these factors inside the organisation, there are additional factors outside of the organisation – the greater environment. The environment, from a leadership perspective, includes such things as the competition, suppliers, legislation impacting on personal, family and business organisation behaviours, and a range of other factors that are 'outside' the organisation itself. These could include such things as building regulations, occupational health and safety legislation, anti-discrimination legislation, minimum wage and employee entitlements, the overall job market, international and national economics, and a myriad other issues that tell us what we may or may not do and how we may or may not do it. The Global Financial Crisis of 2008–2009 focused attention on these outside factors in a way that hadn't been seen since the time of the Great Depression 80 years earlier. ...

In other words, whether or not desired performance is achieved depends on the individual, the organisation, and factors totally outside the organisation. The factors impacting on the individual and the organisational factors can be largely controlled from within the organisation: the environmental factors cannot.

But even the issue of 'willingness' and 'ability' is a little more complex than is often acknowledged. Over the past 40 or so years the motivation industry has emerged. Today it is worth millions of dollars throughout the world. The motivation industry is largely based on the premise that people will be inspired to greater performance through stories of hardship being overcome and success attained. The argument is that people receive a psychological boost through hearing of what others have achieved and how they have done it: that this will inspire them to become similarly successful.

There is an element of truth in this proposition – but it is also open to serious abuse. There are people who become as reliant upon or addicted to 'motivational seminars' as other people do to adrenaline, gambling, alcohol, nicotine and other legal and illegal drugs and activities. These people require a regular 'fix' – generally in increasingly frequent doses (as can sometimes be seen in relation to sales teams where the majority of the remuneration is from commission on sales) – if they are to perform even close to the standards that are desired. To change the metaphor, some people are like campers around a camp fire who vary their distance from the flames depending on whether they are comfortably warm, too hot, or too cold. Without the external stimulus they would be uncomfortable, possibly miserable, and unable to function effectively. …

Most people want to do a good job. Most people want to put their very best in for their organisation. Preventing them are such factors as the quality and quantity of feedback and the stumbling blocks caused by inadequate or inappropriate integration of knowledge, strategy, non-human resources, structure and human process.

What this model does not show, and yet what is also critical if we are to obtain and maintain a high-performing organisation, is that performance is really comprised of at least four integrated components (see below). All too often it seems that these components are treated as though they were discrete units rather than being totally interdependent variables. To obtain and maintain a high-performing organisation we need to consider these both individually and collectively.

Components of Performance:

1. Organisational

2. Unit or Department

3. Team

4. Individual

Then we need to consider the leadership that draws them all together. The following chapters will consider both of these models in depth but, at this stage, they need some basic explanation.

Overall Organisational Performance

In Chapter 2 we will explore the issue of overall organisational performance. The board's role in this is the concern of Sir John Harvey-Jones that is shown at the start. As he rightly points out, ultimately this is the responsibility of the chairman of any organisation. Yes, he or she will rely heavily on the rest of the board and on the executive team, but it is with the chairman that 'the buck stops'.

In a much earlier book[7] I introduced a process that had its genesis in work done by then colleagues of mine, Tero Kauppinen in Finland and Bo Gyllenpalm in Sweden. This is the Vision into Action process (Figure 1.2) that was designed to consider all of the factors involved in setting and implementing performance standards. The key in this process is that it is initially centred on the board and executive team of any organisation. It focuses attention on the macro of performance. It also sets the scene for a collaborative approach which facilitates engagement and accountability at all levels – and both of these are key contributors to the development and maintenance of a high-performing organisation.

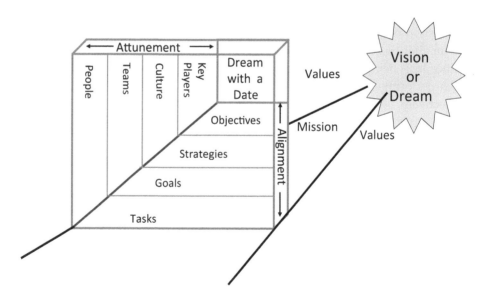

Figure 1.2   The Vision into Action process

7   Long, Douglas G., *Competitive Advantage in the Twenty First Century: from Vision into Action*, CLS, Sydney, 1993.

This process looks at all the variables with which the board and chairman ought to be concerned and, properly implemented, it provides targets and guidelines for every person at all levels and in all areas of any organisation and leads to a natural hierarchy of performance as shown in Figure 1.3. As stated above, this Vision into Action process will be fully explained later (Chapter 2), but it is shown here to stress that, in the quest for high performance, it is impossible to overemphasise the importance of considering both the short-term and the long-term viability of an organisation and both the 'hard' and 'soft' side of the organisation. Too often the emphasis is primarily on the short term and the 'hard' side – quarterly reporting and the annual results that are linked to executive bonuses – with the result that, in the long term, the performance of the organisation is seriously impeded.

During the 1980s the concept of 'quality' became a key area for organisational improvement and productivity gains. Probably the best known exponent of the quality approach was W. Edwards Deming[8] and the concepts propounded by Deming and others are widely known and implemented to the stage where 'quality' is now largely a 'taken as read' concept by many organisations. Central to the quality concept is the belief that the critical area for improvement is 'the system'. Quality approaches largely recognise that there are two causes of quality problems – systems causes and special causes. By shifting emphasis away from the 'special causes' (which often will recur no matter what is done because the underlying issue has not been addressed) to the system or process which drives all outputs it becomes possible to bring about lasting improvement and real change. This is the emphasis of the Vision into Action process and of the Leadership for Performance model. Only when the entire system – the organisation in its entirety, is creating the right environment for people at all levels to be successful can there be a high-performing organisation. The Leadership for Performance model coupled with the Vision into Action process brings about a leadership systems approach to obtaining high performance.

Of course, in using this approach the distinction between 'open' and 'closed' systems must be understood. Systems theory argues that there is a continuum between open and closed systems. The characteristics of a closed system are that all factors can be identified and/or accounted for in the model; that outcomes are predetermined; accordingly all planning can be predictive; and, generally, that the model can be expressed mathematically. By contrast an open system's characteristics are that no matter what is done there will always

---

8   See, for example, Deming, W. Edwards, *Out of the Crisis*, Cambridge University Press, Cambridge, 1986.

be some outside factors that cannot be identified at the outset; that outcomes are a working hypothesis; accordingly all planning must be descriptive; and, generally, the model must be expressed verbally.

The Vision into Action process operates on the premise of every organisation being an open system that is constantly impacted by forces beyond the control of the board, executive or management – the external environment factor of the Leadership for Performance model. Today it is a very brave (or very stupid) person who seeks to operate an organisation (or any part of it) as though it were a closed system. This is true whether we are talking about large or small, public or private, for-profit or not-for-profit organisations. Consequently organisations must be constantly open to the need to change direction and refocus. This is a key element of the Vision into Action process and it is one of the most important reasons why revisiting the whole process at least every three years is so vital.

In understanding the Vision into Action process it must be stressed that different levels within an organisation, while being impacted by the whole process, have different responsibilities for its implementation. This is illustrated in Figure 1.3.

• Chairman	–	total responsibility including the culture
• Board	–	vision, values, mission, dream with a date, governance
• CEO	–	dream with a date, operational performance
• Executives	–	dream with a date, objectives, strategies
• Managers	–	goals, tactics, roles, responsibilities
• Other Employees	–	tasks

Figure 1.3   The hierarchy of organisational performance

High-performing organisations know that unless the right environment is established and maintained by the board and executive, then managers and other employees cannot be expected to perform to their best. How to develop this right environment will be explored in Chapter 2.

Unit/Department Performance

In Chapter 3 we will explore the issue of operational unit or department performance. In this section we will consider:

- the 'Mini Org';

- research and diagnosis;

- 'Version of the Vision';

- executive responsibility;

- cooperation with other units/departments;

- leading change;

- coaching for performance.

The focus here moves away from the organisation overall and from the role of the board and chairman, to the role played by executives and managers. This chapter explores the crucial question of how executives and managers can really 'add value' to the entire organisation as well as to the work done by the people who answer to them. How do (or should) executives and managers develop and implement the structures and policies, the tactics and roles, which will encourage success?

It is very important – though often omitted – to deal with these issues that should be the domain of the executive in any organisation. In today's dominant organisational approach, the emphasis is on power, authority and control. Most of those at the top of organisations are understandably concerned about anything that might impact negatively on their total remuneration package. While this may not be overtly expressed, the fact remains that for most executives total remuneration package is an underlying, covert concern – and, given the way organisations are currently run, one that is totally legitimate. But a lot of the current way we use power, authority and control may actually be counter-productive to obtaining a high-performing organisation. This chapter will explore the reasons for this and will provide alternative approaches that can be considered.

Team Performance

In Chapter 4 we will explore the responsibility of managers – the issue of team performance. If one reads much of the literature – especially in the 'popular' genre – it would appear that all teams are basically the same. This leads to the conventional wisdom about teams seeming to be that:

- 'teams' are always 'the way to go';

- a 'team' will usually give a better result than individuals;

- sending individuals on 'team building' exercises will help the team perform.

In this section we will also explore the team performance curve (Figure 1.4).

The team performance curve will lead us to also consider that:

- a 'group' is not a team – so what is the difference?

- teams are not always the answer and why;

- teams do not automatically perform;

- there is a 'death valley' with teams;

- developing a high-performing team is hard.

While not providing any form of team-building concept (there are plenty of those readily available from a wide range of sources), this chapter will explore the issue of creating an environment in which teams can become fully effective and in which they can contribute to developing and maintaining a high-performing organisation. It will be shown that the formation and use of teams should be the responsibility of managers who are operating in a supportive environment created by the organisation's executive.

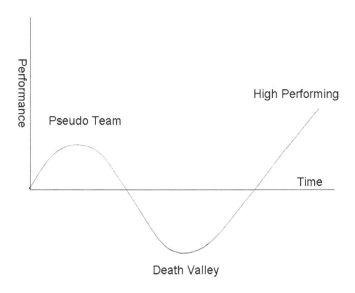

Figure 1.4   The team performance curve

Individual Performance

In Chapter 5 we will explore the issue of individual performance – including a new look at the sometimes vexed question of performance management and performance appraisal.

Individual performance is dependent upon two things:

1.   the individual's competence and motivation – their capability;

2.   the environment within which they operate.

And this is true no matter at what level the individual is found.

The fact is that most people, no matter where they may be in any organisation, want to do a good job. Almost invariably, when they fail to meet performance standards the real cause fault lies not with the individual but in factors beyond their control. It's back to the point made by Sir John Harvey-Jones: failure in performance indicates a failure in leadership – ultimately a failure by the chairman. In this chapter you will be introduced to practices that can impact positively on individual performance by creating an environment that is highly conducive to individual success – and that starts with recruitment and induction then moves to the matter of developing and implementing a new form of performance appraisal system – and one that has been proven to be totally effective.

Leading the High-performing Organisation

At the heart of the Leadership for Performance model is found 'leadership'. There are myriad leadership models and approaches in use today and every organisation will have its own approach which may or may not be based on one of these well-known models. Third Generation Leadership does not advocate any specific leadership model – rather it focuses on the mental approach (our brain's locus of control) that affects how we implement the model(s) being used by our organisation. The critical thing is not so much the approach or model that is being used, rather it is the way in which any model is implemented – because most approaches and models can be used in a positive manner that grows both people and the organisation or in a negative way that is manipulative and ultimately destructive.

In this chapter we will consider what lies behind whatever leadership approach or model we use – our brain's locus of control[9] – and we shall explore ways of moving our locus of control from the red zone of reaction to the blue zone of innovation, creativity and courage. The red zone–blue zone concept will be explained in this chapter. It will be shown that only when we are operating from the blue zone are we able to fully develop and maintain a high-performing organisation.

Chapter Summary

This introductory chapter has introduced all the concepts that will be addressed in this book. The emphasis is on obtaining high productivity and high performance in all areas and across all levels of any organisation. The complexity with which leaders and managers at all levels in any organisation have to deal is summarised in the Leadership for Performance model (Figure 1.1).

9   The concepts of 'the brain's locus of control' and the 'red zone–blue zone' dichotomy are explored fully in Long, Douglas G., *Third Generation Leadership and the Locus of Control: Knowledge, Change and Neuroscience'*, Gower Publishing Limited, Farnham, 2012.

This model highlights the fact that:

- Developing and maintaining a high-performing organisation requires the ability to understand and deal with different (and increasing) levels of complexity.

- There are four different operational levels on which a high-performing organisation depends – a fault in any one of these can impact negatively on productivity and performance.

- The role of the leadership in every organisation is to consciously create an environment in which high performance is possible – to set people up for success. Leadership is the hub around which every factor rotates.

Taking the First Step to a High-performing Organisation

Consider your own organisation – the one in which you work:

- What are the key performance indicators by which you are assessed?

- How do these link with the vision, mission, values and ultimate objectives of your organisation?

- What is the relationship between your personal performance indicators and the measures by which your manager and the organisation overall are assessed?

- What are the things that make it hard for you to meet your personal performance standards?

- What are the things that make it hard for your organisation to meet its performance standards?

- How would you describe the leadership in your organisation?

- How different are you as a leader from the other leaders in your organisation? Why? Does it matter? Why?

2

Overall Organisational Performance

The entire issue of organisational performance starts with the board and, as the quote from Sir John Harvey-Jones makes clear, 'the buck stops' with the chairman. Ultimately it is the chairman who sets the tone for any organisation. The very first words in this book are a quote from Sir John Harvey-Jones about the role of a company's chairman. I chose this quote very deliberately because it opens a focus on the conflicting roles that are filled by directors – and especially the chairman. But it's not just the chairman who can have conflicting roles.

Every company has three distinct groups of critical internal stakeholders – the shareholders who own the company, the board who, as agents of the shareholders, answer to the shareholders (and that is supposed to mean *all* the shareholders and not just the major ones or various pressure or lobby groups) for the overall governance of the company, and the employees (of whom all executives are a part) who are responsible for the actual work done in and by the organisation. Sometimes these roles compete – for example it is not uncommon, especially in larger organisations, for shareholders to also be employees and sometimes board members – right down to the grass roots of the organisation. However the distinction of roles often seems lost at board and executive level – for example, I have frequently had executives talk to me about 'the employees' as though those at lower levels in the organisational hierarchy are different from themselves. They're not! Executives are also employees even though they may be employed under quite different conditions from those of other people and, from time to time, executives need to be reminded of this. A clear sign that this distinction has been forgotten, in reality even though not in rhetoric, is when the board and executives make decisions that can be seen to primarily benefit themselves rather than the optimum combination of long-term stability and viability of the company along with the short-term returns to shareholders – executive remuneration can be just one glaring example of this.

In today's business environment the conventional thinking seems to be that very high remuneration for executives sets the tone for high performance throughout the organisation. While there is some support for this[1] other studies have questioned this premise. A paper by academics from University of Sydney, University of Canberra and University of New South Wales[2] argued that, in the ten years to 2002, executive remuneration in Australia had increased from 22 times average weekly earnings to 74 times average weekly earnings. The researchers examined three criteria – return on equity, share price change and change in earnings per share. Based on this they concluded that there was no positive link between high executive pay and company performance – in fact their data showed that the performance of a company can deteriorate in direct relation to increases in executive remuneration. They conclude that high excessive pay levels actually coincide with a lower 'bottom line'. Whether or not one accepts their conclusions, their report certainly provides food for thought.

The findings from this study receive some support in the later (2012) work by Chris Stephenson[3] where he quotes one of the executives he interviewed as saying:

> *Are the management team incentivised for strategic thinking? I think not. They're incentivised as everyone's told you by short-term goals. Also, we don't expect to last more than 3 or 4 years in the job so what's our incentive? It's not LTI (long-term investment) it's short-term bonuses; short term survival.*

A September 2012 article in *McKinsey Quarterly*[4] also has implications for any short-term focus that is concerned about the organisation's results primarily during the incumbency of any executive or manager. This article suggests that putting short-term organisational success ahead of long-term organisational health is fraught with danger. Indirectly related to this issue of short-term versus long-term focus is a recent interesting report (January 2012) from the news department of the Australian Broadcasting Corporation.[5] The news item

---

1   See, for example, http://astonjournals.com/manuscripts/Vol2011/BEJ-31_Vol2011.pdf, where a 2011 University of South Carolina study found a positive correlation between executive remuneration and organisational performance as measured by return on equity, April 2011.
2   http://www.parliament.wa.gov.au/intranet/libpages.nsf/WebFiles/Hot+Topics+-+Shields+repo rt+Executive+salaries/$FILE/Buck+stops+here.pdf, 2003.
3   Stephenson, C., *What Causes Top Management Teams to Make Poor Strategic Decisions?*, 2012, thesis for the degree of DBA from Southern Cross University, NSW, Australia.
4   http://www.mckinseyquarterly.com/Retail_Consumer_Goods/Strategy_Analysis/ Encouraging_your_people_to_take_the_long_view_3014, September 2012.
5   http://www.abc.net.au/news/2012-12-11/global-trends-2030-report/4421086, December 2012.

was on a (then) very recent American intelligence report that suggests China will surpass the US as the world's largest economy during the 2020s and that India during the 2030s will be the rising power house that China is today. It quotes the report's principal author, Dr Matthew Burrows as saying, 'If you go from crisis to crisis you increase your risk of going off the rails.' Emphasising the need for the US to make a quantum shift in its thinking and practices, the report goes on to say Asia will overtake North America and Europe combined in global power as its gross domestic product (GDP), population, military spending and technological investment surpasses the West's, but that the US will remain what it calls 'first among equals'. Although this report from Burrows et al. is not agreed with by everyone, clearly in its writers' opinion there is an implication that an emphasis on the relatively short term permeates not just commercial organisations and government agencies but that it reaches to the very top of the USA's overall administration – its Congress and Senate. As the earlier mentioned *McKinsey Quarterly* article made clear – a focus on the long term is vital for success.

Sir John Harvey-Jones's call for attention to the real role and responsibility of boards is echoed in the 2012 article by Michael Useem[6] of Wharton School, University of Pennsylvania when he says that, until relatively recently, it was almost taken as read that the leadership of an organisation, from the board down, would both know what were their real responsibilities and would exercise them. This meant that there was no real need to discuss how boards and executive were operating. He makes the point that the situation appears to have changed and that today there is a very real need to discuss the issue of the board and the leadership of organisations.

While in this paper Useem is not looking specifically at the short-term focus vs. long-term focus dichotomy, he does seem to be to be echoing that concern when he speaks of the board's responsibility 'to ensure that shareholder value is protected and increased'.

The truth is that, to be really successful, an organisation has to perform in both the short term and the long term and, in ensuring this, people at every level must be very careful not to confuse the roles they are fulfilling – in other words, board members, even if they are shareholders, must never lose sight of the fact that, as directors, even though it is the large shareholdings that will probably elect them to the board, they have an equal level of responsibility and accountability to every shareholder no matter how small their stake; an

---

6   http://www.mckinsey.com/features/leading_in_the_21st_century/michael_useem, October 2012.

executive, whether or not a director and/or a shareholder, must never lose sight of the fact that, as an employee, he or she is there to optimise both short-term and long-term performance of the organisation rather than his or her own personal interests and so on. A failure in this concern about either the short term or the long term can mean the demise of the organisation and, as history shows, this, unfortunately, is not uncommon. Consequently every organisation needs an approach that ensures there is an appropriate balance between both short-term and long-term demands and in which the roles being filled at every level are very clear. While there are some measures (such as paying CEO and executive bonuses only on what happens to an organisation in the five years after the CEO leaves the organisation) that would certainly increase the probability that both a short-term and long-term approach receive appropriate attention, most of these are unlikely to be implemented because of the vested interests involved.

This, of course, raises questions as to the most appropriate measures of an organisation's performance and its path towards whatever is selected. In November 2012 *Harvard Business Review* published an article by Colin Price[7] entitled 'Leadership and the Art of Plate Spinning'. This article refers to a book, *Beyond Performance: How Great Organizations Build Ultimate Competitive Advantage*[8] by Price and a colleague, Scott Keller, which used data from over 700 companies and concluded that the traditional approaches to running a company may no longer be the best way of achieving results. The traditional approach has been to focus on financial and operational issues by pursuing multiple short-term revenue-generating initiatives and meeting tough individual targets – quarterly reports to the stock exchange are an obvious driver for this and, for many analysts, these reports are the key data on which to make decisions. Price and Keller suggest that organisations seeking 'superior performance' – in other words 'high-performing organisations' – may be finding that this approach is not the most effective one and they need to find a new way forward. They offer some valuable suggestions as to what this way may be while the Briysun Case Study provides another example of how a totally different approach – Third Generation Leadership – is proving their key to success.

The Vision into Action process that I introduced in Chapter 1 is a key part of this Third Generation Leadership approach. It is a practical and readily

7   http://www.mckinseyquarterly.com/Organization/Change_Management/Leadership_and_the_art_of_plate_spinning_3037.
8   Price, Colin and Keller, Scott, *Beyond Performance: How Great Organizations Build Ultimate Competitive Advantage*, John Wiley and Sons, New Jersey, 2011.

applicable means of finding and implementing a new way forward. This process ensures both the short term and the long term are constantly considered and, in doing this, it ensures that everyone from the chairman down pays appropriate attention to both the 'hard' and the 'soft' sides that are critical to obtaining a high-performing organisation. We will now consider the Vision into Action process in detail.

The Vision into Action Process

As I have already said, the originals of this model were first developed by then colleagues of mine, Tero Kauppinen in Finland and Bo Gyllenpalm in Sweden but the version I am showing here was first introduced by me early in the 1990s on the 'Leadership in Senior Management' programme that I conducted at Macquarie Graduate School of Management until 2001. For some 25 years it has been used by me in the successful transformation of small and large organisations across Australia and the Asia-Pacific region.

VISION

The process starts with a 'vision' or a 'dream'. This is a very broad statement about what the organisation seeks to achieve. It will probably include such words and phrases as 'world-class performer', 'the best', or some other idealistic

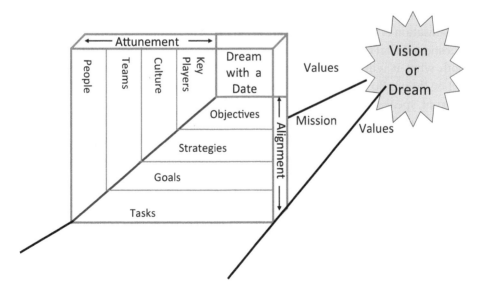

Figure 2.1   The Vision into Action process

terminology designed to position the organisation ahead of any competitor. In many cases this may well be a generic statement and, should they want to take a short cut, a quick search on the World Wide Web will quickly provide any organisation with a variety of choices available for rapid inclusion into any plan or other document. Of course not all organisations will want to take this easy way out and most of those with which I have worked find that spending time really thinking this concept through in detail provides considerable benefit.

From organisations with which I have worked, examples of visions are:

We will be recognised by our customers as a world-class performer and the Australian leader in energy retailing.

We will be a successful, diversified and innovative company that is renowned for integrity, quality and excellence by:

- *meeting customers' expectations;*
- *meeting employees' expectations;*
- *enhancing team work;*
- *being socially responsible.*

MISSION

The next step is to consider what business the organisation is really in and what business it should be in – its mission. This is the road or path along which the organisation is to travel in order to attain its vision or dream. By answering the question, 'What business are we really in?' the organisation is starting to define both what it will be doing and, probably of equal importance, what it will *not* be doing. Bo Gyllenpalm, one of the developers of this Vision into Action concept, speaks of this as 'the cone' of the business – things within the cone will be done whilst things outside the cone, no matter how good and/or important, will not be done by this organisation at this stage in its life even though they may be a legitimate business for some other organisation now or, perhaps, may be legitimate for this organisation at some future stage.

Bo Gyllenpalm's implication that the mission may change is important. It has always been known that organisations may make changes in what they are doing but, in the past, things like long product life cycles and limited competition meant that such changes were considered unlikely or emerged only very slowly. Today's fast moving world with its explosion in technological advancements means that an organisation may need to rethink its core business on a regular basis – failure to do so may mean that the organisation ossifies and dies. Confronting the questions, 'What business are we in now?' and 'What business will we need to be in tomorrow?' could mean the difference between organisational life and death.

From organisations with which I have worked, examples of mission are:

To supply adequate communications to all areas of Papua New Guinea by efficient management of physical, financial, and human resources to provide the PNG Government an acceptable rate of return.

We are an energy retailing organisation.

VALUES

The mission of the organisation is anchored by its values. Values are emotionally loaded beliefs or attitudes. They are those things we consider to be of such importance that we will allow them to dictate how we should behave.

Most organisations have 'values statements' but, too often, these are couched in such generic terms that they provide little or no real guidance as to behaviour because they allow such a broad range of interpretation. One of my highly respected earlier colleagues, the late Major I.V (Ian) Reid RAA, once discovered that some organisations see values as being subject to change when they are found to be inconvenient. After retiring from the Army, Ian was working with an organisation that had 'safety' as one of its values. In one area, outside the flammable goods storage, there was a sign: 'No smoking. Persons smoking in this area will be summarily dismissed'. While Ian was there, a person was caught smoking right beside the sign. It transpired that the offender was both the next door neighbour of the person who caught him and the father-in-law of an executive. Not only was he not dismissed but the sign was changed to read 'No smoking. Persons smoking in this area may be subject to dismissal'! Clearly, in this organisation, 'values' were a moveable feast!

A problem I frequently encounter is 'ambiguity of values'. When I work with organisations I discuss the relationship between the values espoused by the organisation and those I see practiced by its employees at all levels. When a discrepancy is found, a not uncommon response is to receive a shrug of the shoulders and comments along the lines of 'forget what's in the values statement

– this is the way we actually do things here'. And I receive this response from members of the executive group every bit as much as I receive it from people at the 'grass roots' level of organisations. Perhaps that is why an event such as the Global Financial Crisis which started in 2007 elicited such a lukewarm response from the regularity authorities – plenty of noise but, in reality, not much changed. Certainly the economist Paul Krugman,[9] is concerned about this ambiguity when he provides the example of a board seeking to find alternative reasons for awarding their CEO's bonus even though the agreed performance measures were not being met – it appears their emphasis was on keeping the CEO happy by paying the CEO what he thought he was worth rather than on what actually transpired in terms of performance.

An understanding of the real values operating in an organisation is probably the most important critical consideration relating to the future of an organisation – especially if there is a merger or takeover in the offing – because the values we practise – rather than those that are in any values statement – are those that really drive the organisation. What I am saying is, that if you want to know the values of an organisation, look at what is being done rather than at what is being said.

In the organisations I have found to be really 'values driven', the values statements are presented in a behavioural form such as: '*We value our employees. This means that …*' or '*Safety is a key value in this organisation. This means that …*'

I have also found that such organisations don't have a huge list of 'values'. They distil their values to the most basic yet comprehensive form possible so that there are only around five value statements and each of these is supplemented by very clear behavioural implications. The result is everyone can quickly become aware both of the statements themselves and of what they mean in the day-to-day operations. In these cases, it ought to then follow that if any person, from the chairman down, contravenes these values, their on-going employment in the organisation ought to be under serious threat. Perhaps this possibility of dismissal for failure to enact the espoused values is why so many 'values statements' are wishy-washy motherhood statements that can be widely interpreted.

From organisations with which I have worked, examples of values are:

---

9   Krugman, Paul, *The Conscience of a Liberal*, W.W. Norton, New York, 2009.

We care for our people which means that we will provide secure, long term employment for our staff; we will provide fair remuneration to everyone; and we will provide a work environment that is free of prejudice, bullying (physical and/or emotional), and fear; where everyone has the opportunity to experience personal and professional growth; and where they can obtain a sense of achievement and enjoyment in their work.

We will focus on the customer which means that we will at all times treat all customers and prospective customers with absolute respect and our sales approach will be focused on ascertaining and meeting real needs at a price which is both competitive and fair to the customer while providing an appropriate level of return to the company.

DREAM WITH A DATE

When I was in the army there was a joke tossed around about one of our allies. They were said to operate under a 'ready, fire, aim' approach to combat. A similar statement could be made about many organisations when it comes to their sense of direction.

A 'dream with a date' is a sharply focused, quantitative and qualitative description of what an organisation will look like at some finite future time. In my experience this is normally about five years hence. This is your target or your magnetic north – it is something that will continue to give you a clear sense of direction even when everything appears to be disastrous and the excreta is hitting the air conditioning.

To develop this dream with a date, I have found that scenario planning is a valuable tool. Scenario planning consists of developing and considering a range of alternative situations that could pertain in the future. This range of possible 'scenarios' then enables planners to consider how these factors are likely to impact on the organisation. From this base it becomes possible to prepare for almost any possible contingency. The dream with a date should be the best guess stretch target for the organisation over a defined time. It will then need to be monitored regularly and gap analyses done so that there is a good probability of it being attained no matter what subsequent years might bring.

High-performing organisations then revisit this process at least every couple of years so that there is a continual focus on the long term.

From organisations with which I have worked, examples of dream with a date are:

> *By June 30, XXXX we will be the pre-eminent firm for Corporate Recovery and Insolvency work in every State in Australia. We will operate at the upper level of consulting while retaining traditional corporate recovery and insolvency work. Our reputation will be that of leaders in professional standards and services. We will be recognised for our probity.*

> *By June 30 XXXX our revenues will increase by 25 per cent over the YYYY base and our profits will be $ZZZ million. We will be recognised as a model employer that is responsive to the needs of both our people (wherever they may be in the organisation) and the environment.*

Up to this point in the process both the board and the executive team have been involved. The board's responsibility now reverts to oversight and governance. In one organisation with which I worked, the then chairman later made the point that as result of this process, in subsequent years he seldom, if ever, needed to put any matter to a boardroom vote because, despite the breadth of political views and experience represented on the board, there was an absolute unity of purpose and direction which culminated in all targets being met.[10]

The responsibility can now be shifted to the executive team for implementation of the process that will deliver the desired performance – that is, make the dream with a date a reality. The executives' focus will be on a time frame of, probably, about five years and we will consider this in detail in Chapter 3. But before we go there we need to consider some other elements of the Vision into Action process.

OBJECTIVES

This is the stage at which a modified traditional business planning process comes into play. But in this Vision into Action process the executives start at the future desired state – the dream with a date – and make their way back

---

10 Moyes, Allan G., *For Sale: Quality Leadership*, CLS, Sydney, 1997.

to the present rather than starting with the present reality and determining what should be done. Starting from the dream with a date, the executive team now work backwards to set business objectives on both an annual and a divisional basis. If you like, they are 'reverse engineering' the dream with a date so as to avoid constraining themselves by what they perceive to be current limitations. Their effort is spent working out how something can be done rather than in justifying current constraints that might focus on why something might *not* be done.

STRATEGIES

One of the advantages of this 'reverse engineering' approach is that it tends to encourage innovation and creativity in the entire planning process. In terms that I introduce in *Third Generation Leadership and the Locus of Control*[11] it fosters and maintains a 'blue zone' brain approach (see Chapter 6) rather than remaining primarily in the 'red zone' of experience and, all too often, of self-imposed or other limitations. This is especially important when we reach the issue of strategies.

Strategy can be defined as 'the determination of courses of action designed to facilitate the achievement of objectives and goals'. It is a high-level consideration of the best way forward – the way with the highest probability of achieving desired targets.

Gary Hamel, a well-respected researcher in the strategy field, has a website[12] where he places items to stimulate thought. In November 1997 one such article was headed 'The search for strategy'. In this Hamel said that the concept of strategy had changed and that strategy no longer required a disproportionate share of executives' attention. He went on to argue that we need to move away from some traditional aspects of strategic planning to strategic orientation and strategic thinking. In other words, let's understand where we want to go and the general route that will be taken to get there, but let's also realise that there are myriad factors which will impact so we must adjust and adapt to meet these on our journey. In this concept, once strategic orientation is known, 'strategy' per se emerges.

---

11 Long, Douglas G., *Third Generation Leadership and the Locus of Control: Knowledge, Change and Ueuroscience*, Gower Publishing Limited, Farnham, 2012.
12 http://www.garyhamel.com/ and http://strategos.com/, Novermber 1997.

Hamel went on to state:

> *Strategy is always the product of a complex and unexpected interplay between ideas, information, concepts, personalities and desires ... Foresight doesn't emerge in a sterile vacuum: it emerges in the fertile loam of experience, coincident trends, unexpected conversations, random musings, career detours and unfulfilled aspirations. But the question remains, can we do anything to increase the fertility of the soil out of which strategy grows? Can we make serendipity happen? Or at least encourage it? Can we prompt emergence? I think so.*

He then suggested that for this to happen, organisations need to listen to new voices, to have new conversations, to view new perspectives, to develop new passions and to be active in experimentation. As he said

> *... opportunities for strategy innovation don't emerge from sterile analysis and number crunching – they emerge from deep experiential learning.*

Ultimately, said Hamel:

> *The goal is not to develop 'perfect' strategies, but to develop strategies that are directionally right, and then progressively refine them through rapid experimentation and adjustment.*

It is this 'strategic orientation' to which the Vision into Action process refers when it lists the issue of 'strategy'. At its core, strategic orientation centres around three main areas – customer focus, product focus and 'this-organisation' focus. In other words we are trying to meet the real needs of the customer; we are trying to promote our product whether or not there is a current demand for it; or we are focusing on what we need as an organisation regardless of anything else. At varying stages in its life cycle, all organisations can and will use any combination of these. It is important to note, however, that strategies are a broad-brush approach rather than detailed plans. It has been suggested that 'strategic planning' is actually an oxymoron as plans fall out of the strategic orientation rather than being part of the strategy. This is something to which Henry Minztberg[13] in his classic work drew a clear distinction when he discussed deliberate strategy and emergent strategy. Minzberg's distinction of the two is clearly endorsed by Hamel and others concerned with the obtaining and maintaining of high-performing organisations.

---

13 Mintzberg, Henry 'Patterns in Strategy Formation', *Management Science*, Vol 24, No. 9, 1978.

High-performing organisations focus on strategic orientation rather on complex and detailed strategies. In my experience, most high-performing organisations have very slim volumes when it comes to their strategies – they know that versatility will be required as reality encounters planning in the achievement of results, and the nominating of 'strategies' is the starting point for the journey – they show the general direction rather than the detailed route.

Providing the earlier steps have been properly followed then the issue of strategy is not difficult – it will naturally fall out of the values and the dream with a date. For example, in the organisation where one of the values was:

> **We care for our people** *which means that we will provide secure, long-term employment for our staff; we will provide fair remuneration; and we will provide a work environment that is free of prejudice, bullying (physical and/or emotional), and fear; where everyone has the opportunity to experience personal and professional growth; and can obtain a sense of achievement and enjoyment in their work*

then clearly one strategy will relate to empowerment of staff.

Similarly, in the organisation that had a value:

> **We will focus on the customer** *which means that we will at all times treat all customers and prospective customers with absolute respect and our sales approach will be focused on ascertaining and meeting real needs at a price which is both competitive and fair to the customer while providing an appropriate level of return to the company,*

one would expect to find strategies that were very customer orientated.

STRUCTURE

At this point it becomes critical for the executive to re-examine the structure of the organisation to ensure that it is supportive of the strategies. The traditional business planning approach (in fact even if not in rhetoric) tends to operate under the premise that the existing structure is appropriate and immutable. This can result in a 'new wine into old wineskins' situation in which the full gamut of possible strategies is not explored and in which, despite what may be said, the organisation continues following its old paths no matter what the future imperatives may be – and, consequently, where high performance is a random end variable! For one international organisation with which I worked, the Vision into Action process led to a realisation of the dysfunctional conflict that existed between various areas of the company – something easily seen by any outsider as well as those at the lower echelons of the company but to which the executive had previously turned a blind eye. Once the executive acknowledged the problem and could look at it in a different way, they could find an innovative way to address it. In this case their solution was to shift all executives to areas with which they were not familiar (finance to marketing, marketing to production, and so on) – on the surface a very high-risk approach – and, in this case, such a radical approach proved spectacularly successful as the executives found they really did have to work as a fully interdependent team in order for any of them to achieve desired results.

The work of Elliott Jaques is important when we consider structure. Jaques[14] developed the concept of 'time span of capacity' which argues that, for maximum benefit to an organisation, people at different levels or 'strata' should have the ability to deal with different levels of conceptual and practical complexity. Jaques argues that the higher one is in the organisational hierarchy, the greater is the need to be able to deal with high levels of complexity and ambiguity – in other words, the practice of leadership goes through a series of qualitative shifts as one progresses up an organisation's hierarchy. As both the Leadership for Performance model and the Vision into Action process make clear, developing and maintaining a high-performing organisation requires this ability to deal with high levels of ambiguity and complexity – something that, far too often, appears not to be the case in a lot of organisations.

It is well known that all organisations go through what is termed a 'life cycle' and the strategy–structure issue is extremely important to optimising this life cycle. One very well powerful life cycle model is that developed by the Adizes organisation[15] (Figure 2.2) which argues that a high-performing organisation needs to optimise the duration of its time at 'prime'.

---

14 Jaques, Elliott, *Time Span Handbook*, Heinneman, London, 1964. See also Jaques, Elliott and Clement, Stephen D., *Executive Leadership, A Practical Guide to Managing*, Basil Blackwell, Inc., Cambridge, MA, 1991 and Jaques, Elliott, *Requisite Organization: A Total System for Effective Managerial Organization and Managerial Leadership for the 21st Century*, 2nd edn, Cason Hall and Co, Arlington, VA, 1998.
15 Full information is available from http://adizes.com. On this website they offer organisations a free diagnostic as to their location on the life cycle as well as being available for assistance in dealing with any issues.

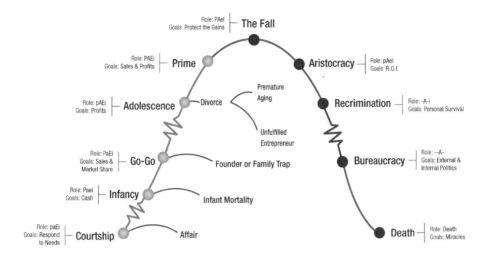

Figure 2.2   Adizes life cycle of an organisation

Source: Reproduced with kind permission from the Adizes Institute.

The earlier stages of their model show the steps to reaching 'prime' – the development of a significant, complex, high-performing organisation – while the later stages of their model show the decline that sets in once 'prime' is passed. The Adizes model also shows the traps that can stop an organisation from reaching prime together with the warning signs surrounding these traps.

Unfortunately many people responsible for the success of organisations fail to take these issues into account. In his research, Chris Stephenson[16] encountered this and it is summarised in the comment by one of the people he interviewed who said:

> *Quite often we [CEOs] know that it's the wrong decision … [but] we have a set of instructions, we have a set of deliverables and we know it can't be done … but it still has to be done – you're told 'just do it!' I'm told to cut my costs by 20 per cent and I know I can't do it because I'm already lean – the only way to do it is to cut into muscle and that means I won't be able to close deals in 6 months time. The board knows the impact but the financial release to the market is coming up in a few weeks and that means I have to cut [to meet market expectations]. As a CEO, you're between a rock and a hard place.*

16 Stephenson, Chris, *What Causes Top Management Teams to Make Poor Strategic Decisions?* 2012, thesis for the degree of DBA from Southern Cross University, NSW, Australia.

Failure by boards to understand and deal appropriately with the levels of ambiguity and complexity necessary for the achievement and maintaining of a high-performing organisation reverberates throughout the organisation and can lead to its demise well before it ought to have traversed its natural life cycle.

One key part of the structure issue relates to the issue of whether or not 'teams' are appropriate (an issue with which we will deal with in Chapter 4) and another key part relates to decision making. Again, Stephenson's work has particular reference here because, as he found:

> *Research shows that high-performing organisations successfully make and implement good decisions. This indicates that good strategic decisions and their effective implementation provide a competitive advantage that directly leads to superior organisational performance. Indeed, when top management teams (TMTs) make strategic decisions, they are potentially conducting the highest leveraged activity they can for an organisation. Considering that strong strategic decision making and execution capabilities are an organisational competitive advantage and represent activities of the highest value to which TMTs can contribute, it seems counter-intuitive that only around fifteen per cent of organisations have the ability to make and implement important decisions effectively.*

There are two distinct yet related aspects to effective decision making in an organisation. The first is the issue of executive decision making that was studied by Stephenson. His work makes clear that the best executive decisions are made when there is a positive decision-making environment. He finds:

> *... direct feedback from CXO (Executive Officer) level participants indicated that a clearly articulated and robust organisational decision-making framework encompassing decision ecosystems, decision leadership and decision governance creates decision equilibrium and yields good strategic decisions.*

> *Direct feedback also indicates that poor decision making by TMTs is mostly attributable to utilisation of weak decision-making frameworks that fails to create decision equilibrium, leading to a decision vacuum of uncertainty and ambiguity. In a decision vacuum, participant feedback shows that decision politics become paramount and take control –*

strategic decisions become highly subjected to human limitations of dealing with complexities and natural self-interest.

Executives are exposed and vulnerable in their roles, and high levels of uncertainty and ambiguity cause them alarm, which both encourages and facilitates them to become risk averse. They become preoccupied with self-interests and bunker down to minimise their exposure to potentially bad outcomes through tactics such as loss avoidance, accountability avoidance and risk avoidance, thereby undermining decision making.

Creating and maintaining decision equilibrium is the responsibility of the decision leader, typically the CEO. Consequently, failure to maintain a decision equilibrium represents leadership failure.

Direct and consistent participant feedback indicates that most organisations do not achieve a state of decision equilibrium, which consequentially leads to decision vacuums that in turn promotes the emergence of decision politics as the basis for strategic decisions.

Politics driving strategic decisions rather than driven by the best interests of the organisation is the main reason for consistently poor strategic decision making by TMTs.

The second is the issue of lower-level, operational decision making. The quality of this is, to a large extent, dependent upon the quality of executive decision making. If the decision-making environment is 'right' at the top then there is a high probability that it will be 'right' throughout the organisation. In high performing organisations, decision making is delegated to the lowest possible level and the parameters within which any person, at any level, can make and implement a decision are known and respected. In addition, in a high-performing organisation, when a decision turns out to be 'wrong' the decision maker is not punished but rather the opportunity is taken for individual and organisational learning and growth. When the fear of negative consequences is removed from the decision-making process, people are far more likely to acknowledge concerns at an early stage so that, if necessary, appropriate and timely remedial action can be taken. The end result becomes a highly effective decision-making process that helps develop and maintain a high-performing organisation.

POLICIES

The next stage in this process involves a re-examination of the organisation's policies – what is the impact of the objectives, strategies and structure on existing policies and vice versa. As with structure, very often policies are assumed to be appropriate just because they have worked in the past. Yet changing conditions may require new and different policies as old policies cease to be relevant or, as may happen, for example, in such areas as employment and safety, failure to revise policies may result in the organisation being prosecuted for legislative violations. It follows, of course, that any policy review must be accompanied with ensuring both that the new policies are known throughout the organisation and that they are fully implemented.

GOALS

The emphasis now shifts to the management team (see Chapter 4) as they become responsible for developing and implementing the organisation's strategy on a day-by-day basis – the application of tactics. This is the stage at which the dream with a date, the objectives and the strategies get broken down into 'bite-sized pieces' that can be assessed and monitored on a daily, weekly, monthly or quarterly basis. This is the point which roles can be assigned to people and the different roles that are needed can be ascertained, defined and filled.

TASKS

All too often organisations run quickly to allocating tasks after they have determined the various objectives to be achieved. This is why, in many organisations, people are somewhat bemused as to the real purpose of their jobs and, frequently, it is the cause of 'looking busy' rather than actually performing work that needs to be done.

One of the frustrations that exist in many organisations is people being unable to see that what they are doing has any real worth. They are busy doing the work allocated but, so far as they can see, what they are doing has little if anything to do with what really needs to be done – in part this is one of the reasons why so many organisations constantly battle to get necessary paperwork completed. The issue is one of alignment.

Today's workforce is increasingly mobile both because of constant awareness of new opportunities through social media, but also because of the surge in casual and part-time rather than full-time employment as employers seek to cut employment costs. Because it is expensive to recruit and train even casual staff, it is important to retain those staff members that are performing well. One way of helping to retain good staff is to ensure that there is a direct and obvious link between every task and the overall focus of the organisation. If there is no obvious link then the time has come to seriously question whether or not that particular task really needs to be performed – and high labour turnover may be an indicator of this need for alignment. In Chapter 3 we will examine a way of checking this matter of alignment.

Linking with the Leadership for Performance Model

So far, in working through the Vision into Action process we have also touched on some of the areas listed in the underlying concept (Figure 1.1). These areas are shown in Figure 2.3.

But, as explained earlier, it is possible to have the most committed and capable people in the world yet still not achieve performance targets. This is because all organisations (or parts thereof) are open systems and there are always factors that are external to an individual's or team's work area, to the department in which they work, or to the organisation itself. The Vision into Action process speaks of these other factors as being people, teams, organisational culture and key players. The extent to which each of these supports or opposes what

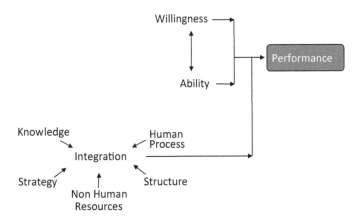

Figure 2.3   Areas for alignment in the Leadership for Performance model

is being done across all levels and areas of an organisation has an immense impact on whether or not performance is attained. It is to these that we shall now turn (Chapter 3) as we consider the responsibilities of the executive.

Chapter Summary

This chapter has explored the link between the overall vision for an organisation and the tasks that individuals are asked to do on a daily basis. It has stressed that:

- ultimately the chairman of any organisation is responsible for ensuring performance is attained;

- there is some debate as to whether or not high levels of executive remuneration actually result in a high-performing organisation;

- an organisation's mission is anchored in its values and for values to be the drivers of performance they need to be expressed in behavioural terms;

- a high-performing organisation starts with its dream with a date and reverse engineers its planning process so as to encourage innovation and creativity;

- people at every level in the organisation ought to be able to see a direct link between what they are doing and what the organisation is seeking to achieve.

Taking the Second Step to a High-performing Organisation

Consider your own organisation – the one in which you work:

- How clear and focused are the vision, mission, values, objectives and goals of the organisation? How can you make them more focused and precise?

- How well known and understood are these throughout the organisation (right down to the grass roots) and what can be done to improve this communication?

- What is the overall vision for your organisation and how does this translate into a 'dream with a date'?

- What are the values on which your organisation operates and how are these expressed in behavioural terms?

- What happens to anyone (from chairman down) in your organisation if they fail to demonstrate these values?

- Thinking about the work that is done at all organisational levels and in all organisational areas, can you see a clear and direct link between these tasks and the 'dream with a date'?

- How are the values, mission, objectives, goals and strategies reflected in the Key Result Areas (KRAs) and the Key Performance Indicators (KPIs) for every area and individual in the organisation? What can be done to improve this linkage?

- If there are blockages in this alignment, where do they occur and what could be done to remove them?

- To what extent does the culture of your organisation support and encourage high performance by everyone? How could this be improved?

3

Unit/Department Performance

Except in very small organisations, people work in a variety of divisions or areas across the organisation. These areas may be functional such as finance, marketing, engineering and so on or more generalist such as maintenance or sales. In medium to large organisations each of these areas or divisions will be the responsibility of an executive whose title will generally reflect both the seniority of the position and the size of the overall organisation.

Many of the issues relating to both individual and organisational performance arise because various departments or areas see themselves as being 'better' or 'more important' than other areas or, in some way, they see themselves as being in competition with other areas or departments. This can lead to dysfunctional activities in both areas.

I have already referred to one example of this (the example where executives were shifted across functional responsibilities), but I also observed it when a property development company decided to operate in an area that was still in property development yet different from their traditional operations. The new operation experienced considerable difficulty in accessing company assets for earthmoving and the like – assets that were temporarily surplus to requirement in the traditional areas yet crucial for the new operation. The result was duplication of expensive, under utilised assets and the development of a lack of trust between the two areas that extended from the executives right down. There was no way by which this organisation could become (or even be described as) high performing while this situation pertained.

The 'Mini' Organisation

Although there can be a temptation for some executives to run their departments or areas as though they were individual fiefdoms, the fact is that each of these is actually a 'mini' version of the overall organisation. If this 'mini organisation' concept was always remembered then much of the in-fighting and squabbling that can occur between departments would be removed. It is part of the Chief Executive's responsibility to ensure that his or her executive group never lose sight of this 'mini' organisation concept.

As I have already indicated, one area in which this fiefdom mentality is often apparent relates to the use of assets. I was consulting to a government organisation in which 'costs' were a major concern and I noticed that one section of the organisation had a huge cost overrun on vehicles because changing needs had meant that more vehicles were needed than had been allocated. Rental vehicles were being utilised to fill the gap. At the same time I saw that other areas of the same organisation had vehicles sitting around unused. I suggested that there was a simple solution to the cost overrun by having the area with need utilise the unused vehicles in the area with excess. I was quickly told (by the CEO no less!) that this was not possible 'because those vehicles have been allocated to specific areas and only those areas are permitted to use them'.

There is no room for fiefdoms or inflexibility in a high-performing organisation. In a high-performing organisation the total emphasis is on the organisation itself and every department or area is recognised both for itself and as a part of the overall organism – a little like an arm and/or a leg being recognised in its own right while simultaneously there being a full recognition that, in order for a person to have total mobility, every limb must function as part of the overall body. Signs of dysfunction between departments or areas are clear indicators that this is not a high-performing organisation.

Research and Diagnosis

The first stage in developing a Third Generation Leadership organisation and implementing a Third Generation Leadership approach is to actually understand the exact problems and issues being faced by the organisation. This requires research and diagnosis – something that otherwise intelligent executives are generally loathe to do on the grounds that 'they know what the problems are'. I always find this response interesting. These are people who, even if generally under duress, will go to a medical practitioner where, no matter what the patient may say in relation to self-diagnosis, the doctor will usually insist on doing his or her own examination so as to ensure that it is the real problem being treated rather than only the symptoms. Yet, when it comes to organisational issues, there is a deep-seated reluctance (or very real fear) to acknowledge that an outside view might actually unearth a different problem from the one the executive thinks needs addressing. The frequently encountered approach from executives could be summarised as: 'Don't confuse me with the facts, my minds already made up!' This myopic approach is directly responsible for many of the instances when problems recur – at the executive's insistence, the consultant has been forced to treat the symptom rather than the real problem.

The education sector is an obvious example of this.

In the early 2000s, John Corrigan of Gr8 Education[1] decided to dedicate ten years to transforming education. He made this decision after participating in a Sydney Leadership Program conducted by The Benevolent Society of NSW where he had become concerned about the issue of the earnings and status of teachers. A study of the available literature indicated that virtually all studies conducted in Australia and overseas sought to ascertain parent, student and community views of teachers and teaching from the base of believing that 'the system' was fine and that the problems, if any, were caused by teachers, parents and a decline in community values. Pressure groups of teachers, parents and others then sought to validate their own position with the result that conflict focused on peripheral or, in Deming's terms, 'special' causes or issues such as remuneration, school conditions, funding and curriculum rather than confront the system's problems. A loop had developed which resulted in a downward spiral of confidence in teachers and the state education system and allowed bodies with vested interests (such as the non-government school system) to flourish even though, in fact, the education provided by non-government schools was not appreciably better (in real terms) than that of government schools.

Corrigan decided to challenge this. An approach was needed that had no a priori assumptions as to the causes of the problem and which would seek to discover causes and solutions whether they were 'systems' issues or 'special' issues – ideally it should combine qualitative and quantitative approaches.

---

1   Information relating to this is available at http://www.gr8education.com and a summary of the research is provided in Long, Douglas G., *Third Generation Leadership and the Locus of Control: Knowledge, Change, and Neuroscience*, Gower Publishing Limited, Farnham, 2012.

The decision was made to:

- investigate a real situation in a school that acknowledged there were problems in student behaviour, school attendance and academic results to get an indication of what the real issues might be;

- get hard data as to perceptions of 'good' teachers and schools;

- using an action research approach, validate these opinions within the broadest possible base of schools and parents;

- based on this data, develop an approach for remedying the situation and trial this with schools across every socio-economic strata.

In 2004 a market research company was commissioned to conduct an Australia-wide random survey of parents, teachers and students asking each person surveyed to describe their ideal school and their ideal teacher. The data from this were then subject to factor analysis and from this three questionnaires were developed – one each for parents, teachers and students.

The questionnaires were then used in an action research project to ascertain the real issues involved in transforming education. This research ascertained that the problem was not with the teachers – almost every teacher was clearly doing what they had been trained to do although, as with any profession, there were varying degrees of quality with which they did this. It was clear that the reasons why education and educators were in their current state were all systems problems and a key part of this was (and is) that teacher training programmes, while doing an excellent job of teaching curriculum and pedagogy, were failing to help teachers develop in their personal engagement skills. Once this was recognised it became possible to provide a cognitive coaching approach that had a direct impact on how teachers interacted with each other and with their students with the result that student outcomes improved considerably from both an academic and a behavioural perspective.[2]

My medical practitioner friends tell me that treatment without diagnosis is malpractice. They point out that although patients may self-diagnose using the internet and/or other resources, because of their proximity to the problem, it is usually hard for a patient to pick up the more subtle indicators of a problem

---

2   A summary of this research is found in Long, Douglas, G., *Third Generation Leadership and the Locus of Control: Knowledge. Change and Neuroscience*, Gower Publications, Farnham, 2012.

and it is easy for them to get sidetracked into believing that they are suffering from one disorder when the truth is that the root cause of the symptom is quite different. Hence some research and diagnosis is vital if the patient is to have a full recovery. Organisations are no different. Executives want to believe that they know the problem but the evidence is clear that time and again they engage consultants to treat symptoms rather than causes; to treat special causes rather than systems causes – because at least this shows something is being done and a quick fix just might eventuate – or at least justify their bonus this year!

Third Generation Leadership is not a quick fix. Obtaining a high-performing organisation is not a quick fix. This was something that Harry and Brian at Briysun had to come to grips with and, although it was difficult for them at the start, the results achieved make it very clear that starting with a thorough diagnosis laid the base for the comprehensive change and improvement that then occurred.

Version of the Vision

Once the diagnosis phase is completed, to assist each division in its overall identification with the entire organisation it can be helpful for each division or area to develop its own 'Version of the Vision'. In this process each executive works with his or her direct reports to work through the Vision into Action process as it applies to their own area.

As an illustration of this, in the organisation with the vision:

> *We will be a successful, diversified and innovative company that is renowned for integrity, quality and excellence by:*
>
> - *meeting customers' expectations;*
> - *meeting employees' expectations;*
> - *enhancing team work;*
> - *being socially responsible.*

Each division or area would start by identifying its customers (for many areas these 'customers' will be internal), then ascertaining these customers' real needs and expectations, then using these data to develop a localised dream with a date. Out of this would then fall departmental objectives, strategies and goals – each of which will be a subset of those pertaining to the organisation overall.

The first strength of this approach is that there is now a clear linkage between what the organisation overall is seeking to achieve and the work being done by each department or area. A second strength is that it places attention on the entire organisation at the same time as it focuses on what each department or area is doing. This is a big step towards the removal of any fiefdoms. Departments are reminded that they are part of a bigger whole – they are interdependent, not independent, entities.

Executive Responsibility

The key task of executives will then move to creating an environment in which their unit or department can be successful. I see this as *the primary executive leadership role* yet it is one which is often forgotten because, no matter the rhetoric, the traditional emphasis has tended to be almost exclusively on the right hand side of the Vision into Action process – the 'hard' aspects of an organisation (objectives, strategy, goals, tasks) – rather than the left hand side of the process – the 'soft' aspects – (key players, culture, teams, people) receiving a similar degree of emphasis. The earlier referred to message from the September 2012 report by *McKinsey Quarterly*[3] is important here. As they point out, you cannot adequately focus on both the short-term and the long-term performance of an organisation unless the 'soft side' – the right hand side of the Vision into Action process – receives plenty of attention.

KEY PLAYERS

The poet John Donne once wrote that 'no man is an island'[4] and that timeless statement is as true today of organisations as it is of individuals. The Vision into Action process recognises this truth and so forces attention to those people and organisations that will have a significant impact on whether or not either individual or organisational performance is attained. The Global Financial Crisis that started in 2007 focused attention on the impact that these outside forces can have in a more graphic way than had been experienced by organisations for decades.

---

3 http://www.mckinseyquarterly.com/Retail_Consumer_Goods/Strategy_Analysis/ Encouraging_your_people_to_take_the_long_view_3014, September 2012.
4 Donne, John (1572–1631), *Devotions upon Emergent Occasions and Seuerall Steps in My Sicknes –Meditation XVII*, 1624.

The starting point in relation to these influencers is to make a list of all the key players that have any potential to influence performance. Ultimately this potential influence may be positive, negative or benign but, at this stage, they should be listed in some neutral way so that later assessment can be made. The important thing is to make a comprehensive list before any form of assessment is made.

This list can then be assessed using some form of analysis such as that propounded originally by Kurt Lewin[5] in his concept of 'force field analysis'. The intention is to rate the extent that each of these parties supports or opposes the path that an organisation wishes to take. In Lewin's approach, once the analysis has been made, decisions can be made as to how best to deal with each of the factors in order to enhance the probability that desired outcomes can be obtained. Some people find Lewin's approach difficult to apply but familiarity with Lewin is not an issue. Other approaches can give very similar data. The important thing is to do a thorough analysis so that you are provided with information that can enable you to decide how to deal with each factor.

CULTURE

The next stage is to reassess the culture of the organisation. In broad terms, 'culture' can be defined as 'the way we do things around here.' Every organisation (like every family) has its own culture – their way of doing things.

Culture per se is neutral – it is neither 'good' nor 'bad' – it's partly your culture that has got you to wherever your organisation is today – because your culture has dictated much of the way in which everyone in the organisation has performed up to this point in time. The question is: is your current culture appropriate for taking you where you need to be in order to make your vision a reality – and is it supportive of a high-performing organisation?

The fact is that when strategy and culture clash, a gap opens up and this gap must be dealt with if a high-performing organisation is to be attained. There is plenty of data to show that when culture and strategy clash, invariably culture wins – and this can spell the demise of the best strategies despite the most ardent efforts of the executive.[6] Failure to deal appropriately with culture

---

5   Lewin, Kurt, 'Defining the 'Field at a Given Time', *Psychological* Review, Vol. 50, 292–310. Republished in *Resolving Social Conflicts and Field Theory in Social Science*, Washington, DC: American Psychological Association, 1997.

6   See, for example, http://www.strategy-business.com/article/19868?gko=04205&cid=20130115e news&utm_campaign=20130115enews, July 1, 2001,Third Quarter 2001, Issue 24.

issues is why it is not uncommon to find an organisation reverting to previous behaviour patterns long after a change programme is considered to have been fully implemented.

One of the best resources I have found on this issue of culture is the work of John Kotter and James L Heskett.[7] They talk of culture as existing on two levels – the group behaviour norms which are visible and relatively easy to change and those which are not readily visible – the shared values – those concerns that are shared by most of the people in a group – and which are harder to change. They go on to make four key points:

- corporate culture can have a significant impact on a firm's long-term economic performance;

- corporate culture will probably be an even more important factor in determining the success or failure of firms in the next decade (that is, in the twenty-first century);

- corporate cultures that inhibit strong long-term financial performance are not rare; they develop easily even in firms that are full of reasonable and intelligent people;

- although tough to change, corporate cultures can be made more performance enhancing.

It can be argued that *the* critical executive responsibility in creating an environment for success is to ensure that the area for which he or she is responsible has a culture that is supportive of the strategies planned and being implemented. At the turn of the twenty-first century, two well-renowned researchers, Michael Beer and Nitin Nohria, made the point that their studies indicated some 70 per cent of all change programmes fail[8] and I am not aware of any variation in that percentage over more recent years. Beer and Nohria suggest that this is because organisations fail to simultaneously deal with both the hard side and the soft side of the organisation – executives seek to force through determined strategies regardless of what this does to the organisation in the long term. Both this figure of 70 per cent and the need to

---

7   Kotter, John P. and Heskett, James L. *Corporate Culture and Performance*, The Free Press, New York, 1992.
8   Beer, Michael and Nohria, Nitin 'Cracking the Code of Change' *Harvard Business Review*, May–June 2000, p. 133.

approach change differently from what is commonly done is echoed in 2012 by Marcella Bremer in her book *Organizational Culture Change: Unleashing Your Organization's Potential.*[9]

There are many tools available to help you assess the appropriateness of your culture. Which one of these tools an organisation chooses to use (or whether you develop your own) is up to you, but one that is worth at least a look is the one discussed by Marcella Bremer – her Chapter 5 is a good start.

In my experience high-performing organisations have quite rapidly emerged when, following an organisational culture analysis, everybody affected is included in focus groups that are held to discuss the best way of moving from the current culture to the desired culture. By ensuring people know why the change is necessary; what the end result should look like; and the part they play in reaching this new situation; the existing organisational culture can be harnessed to support rather than impede the change process. This, of course, may require quite a different leadership approach from what has been extant in the organisation and, in fact, it is one of the reasons why there is such an urgent need for organisations of all types to embrace a leadership approach that brings about engagement of people both with their work and with the other people in their team or work unit. I call this different leadership approach 'Third Generation Leadership'[10] and it is an approach that engenders engagement of people not only with what they are doing but also with each other, their boss and their organisation over all. We will discuss this more in Chapter 6.

The issue here is that executives need to do more than to ensure that there is total alignment on the right hand side of the Vision into Action process so that everyone can see a clear link between what they are doing and where the organisation is going. This alignment issue is no different from what management studies have always been saying should be done. But by itself this is not enough. What the Vision into Action process makes clear is an additional consideration. This additional consideration is that, simultaneous with the alignment aspect, there should be attunement – ensuring that everything is in harmony. My research shows that executives need to ensure that there is also a total attunement both between the organisational culture and the strategies, and between the organisational culture and the people doing the work. In other words, people

---

9   Bremer, Marcella, *Organizational Culture Change: Unleashing Your Organization's Potential*, 2012. OCIA Online, http://www.ocai-online.com.
10   Long, Douglas G., *Third Generation Leadership and the Locus of Control: Knowledge, Change and Neuroscience*, Gower Publishing Limited, Farnham, 2012.

and other 'soft' issues – the attunement factors – are the domain of all executives and they cannot be left to or buck passed on to the Human Resources department.

Executives must deal with both alignment *and* attunement if high performance is to be developed and maintained. A practical way of doing this starts with mapping and flow charting all of the operation's activities.

Mapping and Flow Charting

Quite early in my consulting career – way back in the days before personal computers – I had an assignment with a major property development company. The company had about 450 people in its head office but they assured me they had a couple of spare offices from which I could work and, when I arrived to commence the research part of the assignment, I found this was the case. I went into the allocated office and there on the desk was a couple of those, now old fashioned, folders each about 10 cm thick, containing hundreds of pages of data printed out from the huge main frame computer that sat in its air conditioned sanctuary. I was really impressed with the efficiency of the client because, as I waded through the information, it was clear that much of what I needed to know was right there. For several days I worked through this data, making notes and visiting other people to clarify issues raised, and I felt I was 'getting there'. Then, a few mornings later, I went into the office to find the computer printouts had disappeared – and so had many of my notes that had been written in the margins. My frantic search for the files was disrupted by the appearance of a clerk wheeling a huge trolley on which were piles of computer printouts just like the ones I had lost. He came into the office and placed two more huge folders on my desk saying in passing, 'Oh, I didn't know anyone was in this office these days.' A discussion ensued in which he assured me that he and one other clerk shared the task of distributing computer printouts to allocated locations such as the office I was using and also of removing the old printouts that were out of date. This week it was the other clerk's role to remove the old printouts and it was his task to distribute the new ones. It also became apparent that the office in which I was ensconced had been vacant for months – at least for as long as this clerk had been employed by the client – yet the printouts had been replaced every week or so despite the office being uninhabited. Further enquiries then ascertained that, about three years before, the incumbent of that office had needed the information from the printouts and the IT Department had added this office to their distribution list. Two years ago that person had moved offices but the distribution list had never been updated.

Over the years since then I have often found people doing exactly what they are supposed to be doing – meeting their performance measures to the complete satisfaction of their bosses – yet those things they are doing are unnecessary and/or wasteful. It is clear that it is very easy for once necessary processes and activities to continue long after they have become redundant.

A tool I have found very valuable in determining what needs to be addressed is that of mapping and flow charting every process from the acquisition of resources and supplies through to the depositing in the bank of funds received. There are many ways of doing this but the one I prefer is to start with the CEO and ask him or her to give me an overview of the whole organisational process; then repeat this exercise with each executive but, at this stage, concentrating on their area of responsibility; then to each manager; and so on down to the people who are actually involved in the day-to-day implementation of processes. The beauty of this approach is that it allows an overview of the processes to be obtained before involving people at lower levels in explaining details of the process. Although, as the Briysun Case Study makes clear, this is usually a time consuming and reasonably expensive activity, it is a very powerful approach that removes threat from the upper levels because all they are asked for is an overview while, at the same time, fully involving all lower levels by having them input what they do – in other words, it enhances engagement at all levels because every person in the organisation has some involvement in the process. Once this process is completed it becomes possible to identify any lack of alignment as well as any gaps, duplications and unnecessary activities. It also highlights the need for various areas of the organisation to be interdependent by making it clear that they each rely on other areas to some extent. In the property development company referred to above, this process led to the realisation that (amongst other things) of the 50 or so people (or offices) on the distribution list, the information was required and used by only four or five. Significant cost savings on the stationery budget resulted as well as enabling staff to be allocated to far more productive tasks – a significant impact on productivity and overall performance. In the case of Briysun (as stated in the Case Study) this process was directly responsible for many of the productivity improvements that enabled the profitability turnaround.

Cooperation with Other Units/Departments

A key part of the awareness of attunement is also the cooperation that exists between other units or departments. Quite apart from the key players outside the organisation, among the key players for any area or department are the internal key players – the other areas or departments.

The issue of organisational 'silos' has long been recognised and discussed. In theory it is something addressed in most organisations – in practice, silos remain alive and thriving as I have already illustrated in the earlier examples of dysfunctional behaviour between organisational areas.

I was in an elevator in one of Sydney's major office towers one morning. I glanced around and realised I knew everyone in the elevator – they all worked for the same organisation and most of them even worked on the same floor. There was a shocked and stony silence when I said 'good morning' to them before one person, a divisional general manager, (actually the person I was there to meet) replied with a frosty 'hello'. We reached the departure level, left the elevator and went to her office where it was made very clear to me that company policy was to never talk in elevators. I responded that I knew and appreciated such restrictions applied to gossip or talking about company business but I questioned its relevance both in terms of a general greeting and, more specifically, when everyone in the elevator (apart from me) worked for the same organisation, were not in an organisation in which 'Chinese Walls' were necessary, and they all knew me and my role as a consultant and coach or mentor. (I didn't tell her but in fact I was mentoring or coaching more than half of those in the elevator.) She replied that she had no idea that they all worked for the same company and went on to say, only partly apologetically, that, despite being in her current role for four years, she didn't even know all the 100 or so people in her own department let alone those in other areas! This experience led to some interesting mentoring and coaching discussions with quite a few people that day.

The fact is that every organisation has its formal and its informal structures and both are essential ingredients of a high-performing organisation. While, from an accountability perspective, the formal structure is necessary; it is very often the informal structure that actually gets things done – or not done – as the case may be. In this particular organisation where we had all shared an elevator I had known there was a functioning formal organisation that was hindered by a dysfunctional informal organisation – after this experience in the elevator I had a good idea as to *why* the informal structure was dysfunctional. To a large extent it is in this informal structure that you will often find the 'not readily visible' aspects of organisational culture – the 'real' shared values referred to by Kotter and Heskett above.

In high-performing organisations executives know and appreciate both the formal and the informal structures and they work positively with both of these to heighten the probability that optimum performance will be obtained. This means that the executives need to be constantly moving about the organisation – not to interfere and/or control – but to help remove blockages that are negatively impacting on performance. It was this concept that Peters and Waterman[11] saw when they studied Hewlett Packard and which they termed 'management by wandering around' (MBWA).

All organisational silos invariably become dysfunctional over time. Ageing and a lapse into irrelevance can be a function of all formal structures. All the areas or departments of any organisation need to be dynamic and interdependent. An effective executive in a high-performing organisation ensures that this dynamism and interdependence is both recognised and encouraged.

Leading Change

I have spent most of my working life dealing with change issues and I have led change processes across a variety of organisations – public and private sector; for-profit and not-for-profit; small and large – throughout Australia and South East Asia. Probably the key thing I have learned is that 'leading' change has a far higher probability of the process being successful than has 'managing' change.

While most change starts at the top – either at the executive or board level – it is the executive level that is responsible for actually implementing any change programme. In doing this it is essential that they work both sides of the Vision into Action process. Back in the early 1990s I introduced a model I have found very effective in doing this. I call this 'the cascading manager-once-removed' (Figure 3.1).

---

11 Peters, Tom and Waterman, Robert H. Jr, *In Search of Excellence: Lessons from America's Best-Run Companies*, Warner Books, New York, USA, 1984.

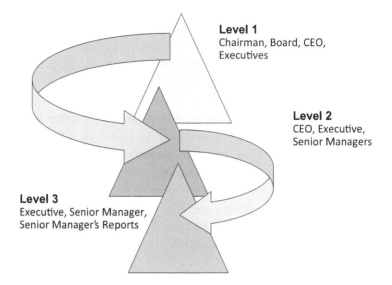

Figure 3.1   The cascading manager-once-removed

I first introduced this model in 1991 when I was working with the board and executive team of a public utility that was being formed through the merger of three smaller utilities. I have since used it with other public utilities, a city council, an oil company in South East Asia, two telecommunications companies, a food-processing organisation, a major financial services company, a professional services firm and a host of small to medium business enterprises. I have found that it does two key things:

- first, it gets all the information disseminated through the organisation very quickly, efficiently and accurately;

- second, it sets up a climate in which people can become committed to the change process.

The model works like this:

Step 1

The board and executive team work together to develop and agree on the vision, mission, values and dream with a date for the organisation and to determine the organisation's basic strategic orientation. During this process, any potential 'ouch points' – things that might derail the change process – are identified and early consideration is made as to how these could be addressed. At the end of this process the CEO designs and distributes a document that goes to every employee explaining what has taken place, the outputs and the process that will now occur. This leads to:

Step 2

Each executive then works with his or her direct reports to, first, communicate the outputs from step 1, then to develop their Version of the Vision; their unit's dream with a date; the actual strategies that they will follow and what these mean for the culture, the structure and the policies in their area. At this stage any clashes with the key players and the culture are identified and concrete approaches for dealing with these are developed. The CEO is present at each of these sessions to show his or her complete endorsement of the process and to provide any further information or to clarify any issues that are assumed to (or actually do) need the CEO's imprimatur.

Step 3

This process is now repeated with each of the senior managers working with his or her direct reports but with the relevant executive being present instead of the CEO. At this stage plans are developed for implementing any actions necessary for dealing with key player and culture clashes and roles and teams are examined to ascertain their suitability for the implementation process.

And so on!

And so the cascading continues to the grass roots level of the organisation with each level considering any 'ouch points' that will impact on them and determining how these should be dealt with.

A clear benefit of this process is that it rapidly becomes an iterative process in which the outputs from each session are disseminated not only down but also across and up so that any potential problems are quickly ascertained and addressed.

In every case, including an organisation of 5,000+ employees and operating over nine sites, this process was able to ensure that everyone was fully informed and involved within eight weeks. The board and executive then had an annual workshop where they jointly examined progress, tweaked the process where necessary, and again cascaded information through the organisation – this time, even in the largest organisation with which I have worked, the cascading process was completed in three weeks. Every three years a new dream with a date was set with each of these providing a five year running target and the cascading process was followed in order to inform and maintain commitment. In every organisation with which I have used this process, the change process has been successful and targeted results have been obtained or exceeded.

The effective implementation of this model requires that the organisation wants to 'lead' change rather than 'manage' change. The difference is that, in 'managing change', there is an attempt to control every (or almost every) part of the process with the upper levels of the organisation's hierarchy determining not only what is to be achieved but, almost right down to the smallest detail, how this is to be achieved – including areas that are not to be considered in the process. In the managing change scenario, despite the appearance of involvement and empowerment of the lower levels, the truth is that real power and responsibility are taken away from those who will be implementing the process. Under such circumstances resistance is invariable and quiet (and sometimes not so quiet) sabotage is not unknown. It seems to me that this is a prime reason why, as Beer and Nohria make clear, some 70 per cent of all change processes fail to fully achieve their desired outcomes.

'Leading' change takes a very different approach.

In all of the organisations with which I have worked on the change process, one of the outputs of the initial board–executive workshop has been a one-page overview of decisions made. This always contains the following as an absolute minimum:

- the vision;

- the mission;

- the values anchoring the organisation (expressed in behavioural terms);

- the dream with a date;

- the strategic orientation.

This is then distributed throughout the organisation in the widest possible way. In a large financial services company with which I worked, not only did every employee receive a hard copy, but a copy was attached to the wall at every level outside every elevator so that not only employees but any person entering or leaving an elevator could see it; in a city council, not only did every employee receive a copy, but a copy was also attached to the fuel pumps where council vehicles were refuelled so as to ensure there was wide discussion; in an oil company, a copy was even sent to every supplier and all major customers. The underlying premise is that the more people who know what we are trying to do, the more likely we are to do it so as to avoid embarrassment. In each case the accompanying memo or letter, jointly signed by the chairman and the CEO, stated clearly that 'this is what we need to achieve and the "what" is not negotiable. What we are now doing is starting a process in which you are invited to help us determine "how" we can and will achieve this.' In several cases this 'what' included the fact that significant staff reductions would occur over a defined period. In other words, there was no attempt to hide any information even though such disclosure might run the risk of causing industrial unrest.

My experience is that this initial communication and at least the first run through the cascading manager-once-removed process invariably meets scepticism, suspicion and at least covert opposition because it cuts straight across the previous experience of almost every employee. But along with this, my experience is that, for most employees, there is also a faint glimmer of hope that something might be different this time. It now becomes vital that this hope is fanned into a flame rather than being extinguished. And that demands leadership!

This 'leadership' must be exhibited in total honesty from the chairman down. Everybody must be told 'the truth, the whole truth, and nothing but the truth'. In one organisation this demand proved too much for the CEO and he eventually left the company because, as the Chairman remarked, the CEO certainly only told the truth, but it wasn't *all* the truth. He consistently omitted telling people things that were important but about which he was scared of the consequences should the truth be known. The result was that these 'sins of omission' later created major problems that eventually called into question the very viability of the company.

Now this does *not* mean that the organisation makes available highly sensitive commercial information that would assist competitors. As a wise mentor once said to me, 'There are some things you know that you tell everybody: there are some things you know that you tell only to those who ask: and there are some things you know that should not be disclosed. Wisdom is knowing the difference!'

What it *does* mean is that you are honest about what can and cannot be disclosed. People always know that some things cannot be disclosed and, in an atmosphere of trust and honesty, they will accept a statement along the lines of 'yes, that has been discussed but, at this stage I'm not at liberty to disclose anything'. Of course, the level of this acceptance is dependent on the extent to which the leader is trusted and respected – secrecy should be used sparingly and only when there are genuinely sound reasons for non-disclosure. Politics and ridiculous levels of secrecy and security will quickly erode trust – just consider the politics of any government where, as we can all see, even despite 'freedom of information' legislation, almost always the attempt is made to ensure the populace are kept in the dark and fed bovine excrement!

In the organisations with which I have worked, this atmosphere of trust and respect starts with respect being shown by the leaders to every person and this respect is partly emphasised by acknowledging every contribution. This has been done by making a summary of every Vision into Action meeting available to everyone involved and rapidly responding with a 'yes', 'no', or 'maybe' to any suggestions or requests together with the provision of the reasons for whatever the response. It also means the rapid implementation of things that have been agreed on together with honest feedback as to the success or otherwise of any agreed initiative. Without exception, in every organisation with which I have worked – whether in Australia or South East Asia – by the end of the second year trust has been at a high level, performance has significantly improved, and intermediate targets either have been met or were well on the way to being met.

As we shall see in Chapter 6, this sort of leadership can be learned and it is very effective in engendering a culture of engagement, accountability, trust and high performance.

Coaching for Performance

Of relatively recent years, the positive impact of coaching in business has become increasingly recognised and widely used. The form of coaching that I have found to bring best results in developing and maintaining a high-performing organisation is 'cognitive coaching'.

Cognitive coaching is different from other approaches because it does not rely on the coach having all the answers – or even any of the answers. It is based on powerful questioning, observational listening and optimistic listening.[12] While mentoring and content coaching require the coach to be more knowledgeable and, usually, more experienced than the person being coached or mentored, with cognitive coaching it becomes a shared journey. In cognitive coaching, the coach works with the other person or people to uncover a solution to which there will be a high level of commitment by both parties. This allows the development of innovative and creative approaches that otherwise might never be considered.

This form of coaching for performance challenges many of our usual stereotypes because it moves us away from any form of a 'boss–subordinate' concept to a collaborative and non-hierarchical approach. It is predicated upon a 'working with' approach in which the coach believes that, under the right conditions, the person being coached will be able to come up with a solution that will work and to which he or she is committed. This sets up the best conditions possible for success to be achieved and, for best results, executives both cognitively coach their direct reports and develop their direct reports to cognitively coach the people who report to them.

THE KEYS TO COACHING AND MENTORING

While coaching and mentoring are separate concepts, they have much in common. No matter whether you see yourself as a coach or a mentor, to be an effective coach or mentor there needs to be trust and respect coupled by appropriate questioning competence and a high level of listening skill.

TRUST AND RESPECT

The days are long gone since there was automatic respect for people in authority – we have been burned so often through the abuses committed by people who have power and authority in every arena of life. Today, more than ever before, a leader increasingly needs to earn the trust and respect of those he or she would influence.

Trust and respect come from two key areas – our expertise and the relationship we have with others. When I was in the army I quickly learned

---

12 There is a broad discussion on this, together with sets of tools, in Mowat, Andrew, Corrigan, John and Long, Douglas *The Success Zone*, Global Publishing, Melbourne, 2010.

to check two things when anyone was talking with me – their rank and their service ribbons – because these would immediately let me know a lot. If a person didn't have a particularly senior rank but their service ribbons showed a lot of active service in combat areas then what they had to say about being a front-line soldier was probably going to be of more practical value than comments from a person with a relatively senior rank but who had never been on 'the two-way rifle range'. A similar situation pertains in all other organisations – someone with an obvious wealth of experience will probably find it a lot easier to develop trust and respect than will someone with only a theoretical understanding of an issue.

But this initial appraisal only opens the door on the speed with which trust and respect may develop. If this initial appraisal isn't coupled with behaviour that demonstrates integrity then the probability of trust developing is low. Accordingly the relationship we develop is crucial – a person with little experience but who can develop strong interpersonal relationships will probably be a more effective coach and mentor than when the reverse pertains.

It is up to the leader to initiate this development of trust – and the key to this is for the leader to demonstrate trust in those being led. Trust has to be earned by leaders – and the starting point for that is for the leader to show unconditional respect to his or her followers.

Most executives find this a little difficult to implement. Our dominant paradigm is power and control. We fight our way up the organisational hierarchy by proving how good we are in comparison with the rest of our peers. We live in a competitive world in which any perceived weakness of dealing with people in order to achieve results could be career limiting – because of this, very often bullying is disguised as 'strong management'. We expect respect by the very fact that our position is proof of our knowledge and experience. The result, all too often, is that we then come across as being 'out of touch' with what is really going on and as being caught up only in our own career – many of us are then viewed as being 'self-centred'. When this happens it is very hard to be an effective coach or mentor. Accordingly we need to learn how to demonstrate respect through a couple of simple behaviours – questioning and listening.

QUESTIONING

The use of questions can be a powerful way of showing people we respect them and that we want to facilitate their development. The trick is to know the sorts of questions to ask – for example there is a huge gulf between the responses that are likely to be obtained if you ask, 'Why did you do it that way?' rather than asking, 'What would you do differently next time, if you could?' The first implies a judgement that is likely to be followed by some form of recrimination so the response will be defensive while the second is likely to generate a thoughtful response that can lead to improvements.

Effective cognitive coaches and mentors use powerful questioning – questioning that elicits reflection and that opens the door to explore new alternatives. This is powerful because it demonstrates respect for what the other person or people know and for who they are. It builds on the adult education premise of starting where a person is currently in terms of knowledge, skill and experience then encourages them to move to a higher plane. Figure 3.2 contains two sets of questions. The first set are questions that are typical of what an executive might ask in today's business environment but, no matter how supportive the executive might try to be, they imply judgment and will elicit a defensive response. The second set is examples of powerful questions that will elicit a thoughtful response.

Which is more likely to elicit a thoughtful response?

Set 1:

- Why didn't you perform as you should?
- Why did this happen?
- Where did it all start to go wrong?
- Why do you think you are no good at this?
- What was wrong with your performance in this area?
- Why did you do it that way?

Or Set 2:

- What aspect of this situation were you happy with?
- What did you learn from this particular situation?
- How would you rate your effectiveness, say, out of 10?
- What rating would you be pleased with?
- What would you need to do to move towards your preferred rating?
- How can you develop strength in this area?

Figure 3.2   Types of questions

In a high-performing organisation, executives learn to use powerful questions and they develop their own sets of possible questions that can be used to help people grow. In a coaching or mentoring situation, the questions that trigger the right responses:

- focus on the other person and their thinking, not the detail in the issue or problem;

- are clear of any attitudes and beliefs of the questioner;

- are easy to understand;

- provide useful (rather than interesting) answers.

Building a repertoire of powerful questions hard wires coaches and mentors for shaping and recall when necessary. Of course, the corollary of this is that, in a cognitive coaching or mentoring situation, the executive needs also to listen in the most effective way. Not listening in the right way to what is being said quickly brings about a scenario in which the would-be coach or mentor is seen as being manipulative and as having a hidden agenda!

LISTENING

Most of us think we are good listeners and we believe that, generally, we respond in the right way to most things people say. However the truth is that there is a variety of ways in which we listen. In *Third Generation Leadership and the Locus of Control* I list ways in which people listen:

- for opportunities to sound intelligent;

- for a chance to say something funny;

- for how I could sound important;

- to information I want;

- to external distractions – other noise, music and so on;

- for what's going on for the other person;

- for approval;

- to my own thoughts, not listening to the other person at all;

- to be able to understand the problem;

- for how I can benefit;

- for the opportunity to one-up the other person;

- for the details so that I can help solve the problem;

- for how I can undermine the other person's point of view or position;

- for how I can change or end the conversation.

Now while these may all be legitimate forms of listening under some circumstances, in a cognitive coaching or mentoring situation they are highly unlikely to produce the desired result. The problem is that, for most of us, whether coach or 'coachee', our thoughts often fit into several categories:

- thoughts that are judging;

- thoughts that are fitting or matching what is being heard into our own previous experience;

- thoughts that are making assumptions (for example, finishing sentences, I know where this is going);

- thoughts that trigger processing (trying to solve the problem, unrelated train of thought);

and none of these really help the other person.

When we want to help someone we are seeking to trigger their engagement in their own thinking and learning. We need to listen:

- without judgement;

- without assumptions;

- for speaker thinking;

- for speaker insights;

- at all levels;

- optimistically.

To do this in a coaching or mentoring situation there are two forms of effective listening:

- **Observation**: listening with the purpose of reflecting back to the speaker what you see and hear.

This shifts listener attention away from internal processing (for example, analysis, judgement and assumptions), that is, away from listener's own thinking and it means that the listener stops doing what is least useful.

- **Optimism**: listening with the belief that the answer will emerge from the speaker.

This focuses the attention of the listener to the speaker's thinking – because that is the only way to solve the problem and it means that the listener starts doing what is most useful.

What I am saying is that authentic and strong attention *on and for the other person* is the underlying social mechanism that triggers engagement and facilitates growth. It is the core of effective mentoring and cognitive coaching.

Chapter Summary

This chapter has explored the role of executives in developing and maintaining a high level of interdependence between the areas or divisions of an organisation. It has stressed that:

- Executives are responsible for creating an environment in which the people at all levels in the area or division can be successful.

- Executives are ultimately responsible for ensuring that all key players are known and for facilitating the process through which positive, negative and benign forces from these key players are harnessed and used.

- Executives are responsible for ensuring both the readily visible and the non readily visible aspects of the organisation's culture are understood and that a culture supportive of the organisation's strategies is in place.

- Executives must ensure both alignment and attunement within their area or division and across areas or divisions in order to facilitate the obtaining and maintaining of a high-performing organisation.

- 'Leading' change is different from 'managing' change – and has a far higher probability of success.

- Cognitive coaching is a powerful tool for facilitating high performance.

Taking the Third Step to a High-performing Organisation

Consider your own organisation – the one in which you work:

- Make a list of all the things that impact on your organisation's ability to operate effectively.

- Sort the list into two groups – those things within your organisation and those things external to your organisation.

- Sort the 'internal' list into the following categories: knowledge, strategy, non-human resources, structure, human process.

- Very honestly and as impartially as possible, assess each item in each category of this list as to whether it actively enhances results, impedes results (usually by causing a problem or blockage that affects some other item from functioning effectively), or operates in such a way as to prevent results.

- Determine how to rid your organisation of those things that prevent results and clear the impediments.

- Determine how those items enhancing results can be further supported.

- Sort the 'external' list into the following categories: those you can influence, those you cannot influence.

- Develop a very clear plan for positively influencing each item you can influence and develop an approach for coping with those items you cannot influence.

- How can you now empower everyone to make the new plan work?

- What are the culture–strategy clashes that could exist? How will you deal with these?

- What coaching and other support will your people need? How are you going to provide this?

- When did your organisation last do a comprehensive mapping and flow charting of every process? How is this kept up to date? What happens with the information from this?

4

Team Performance

For longer than many of us want to remember, the catchword has become 'teams'. And developing and maintaining high-performing operational teams is the responsibility of managers.

It doesn't seem to matter what you read or to whom you listen. Very often people seem to be talking about teams as the key operating unit of an organisation and about empowerment as the way of having these teams function. In fact people now seem to refer to any working group as a 'team' no matter what it is doing or how it interacts.

Several years ago I was presenting a session on leadership to an Advanced Management Programme at a major university. In the course of this presentation I suggested that leadership of teams was qualitatively different from leadership of individuals. In addition I had the temerity to suggest that teams were not always the way to work: that a team decision was not necessarily better than an individual decision: and that, all too often, the chance of synergy occurring was random. To say that this aroused the wrath of at least one of the participants is to be kind. The very clear impression gained was that burning at the stake should be re-introduced with me as its first victim.

Unfortunately, despite the emotional investment in politically correct approaches and the best intentions of many writers, trainers and others, the facts show that, far too often, teams are good in theory but do not work in practice. Because, deep down, most of us know this is true, it is essential that we understand what is involved in obtaining a high-performing team.[1]

In the plethora of books on teams and 'teaming' (that is, developing teams), it is widely shown that work groups *can* effectively accomplish more

---

1   See, for example, http://www.linkedin.com/today/post/article/20130114135908-128811924-one-reason-we-really-hate-teams, January 14, 2013.

than individuals. We know that, through working in teams, employees *can* be more motivated and energised. Each of us has grown up hearing the old adage 'two heads are better than one'. All of these indicators would seem to point the way towards creating teams in order to increase productivity. Yet, as already indicated, our experience indicates that more often than we really like to admit results achieved by teams are different from theory.

Katzenbach and Smith[2] discuss the reasons for this. Their research showed that most people think they know and understand the word *team* yet that very word holds many different personal meanings. Because of this there can be widespread misunderstanding in organisations as to what exactly constitutes a team and how it should work.

In their research, Katzenbach and Smith studied 50 teams working in 30 organisations in the US. One constant they discovered was that teams must have a demanding performance challenge to create and sustain themselves. They found that it doesn't matter whether the performance challenge is identified by the organisation or the team itself. What does matter is that the team adopts it and becomes committed to it.

Much to the chagrin of some trainers and academics, they found also that high-performance teams do not concentrate or focus on the goal of 'becoming teams'. They found that teamwork itself is not the reason for the productivity of teams. Very often those things taught on 'team-building exercises' are not sufficient to ensure team performance. Rather, they found that real teams form best when there are very clear performance demands. Most important, groups of people do not become teams just because they are called teams, or because they are sent off to team-building workshops.

Let me give a very simple example.

Australia is well-known for its frequent bushfires – disastrous fires that, after a series of hot, dry days, can sweep across this broad land, fanned by strong winds and destroying everything in their path. Every few years we get a really bad fire season in which homes are lost, private property destroyed and countless animals – native, farming livestock and domestic – are killed or seriously injured. Often we have people killed by these fires, too. In February

---

2   Katzenbach, Jon R. and Smith, Douglas K., *The Wisdom of Teams: Creating the High Performance Organisation*, Harvard Business School Press, Boston, 1993.

1983 we had one of our worst ever fire seasons that culminated in what have become known as 'The Ash Wednesday Bush Fires'.

February 1983 had been a very hot dry month.[3] Very early in the afternoon of February 16, 1983 I was in Melbourne, working in my office at home, when I noticed the sky, already quite dark because of on-going dust storms over past days, had further blackened and the wind had increased in strength. I turned on the radio and quickly learned that major fires had started across the States of Victoria and South Australia. At that time I had relatively recently left the Army and moved from the Active List to the Active Reserve List of military officers and it was well known that I had extensive experience working with emergency organisations and those who worked for them in a voluntary capacity. Accordingly I was not totally surprised when, a short while later, I received a phone call asking me to report to the State Relief Centre in Melbourne because they were swamped with people wanting to help either through the donation of clothes, food, various domestic goods, money or simply to provide general physical assistance. The State Relief Centre was a relatively small operation in terms of staff and they were unable to cope with the influx of people and material. They needed someone to coordinate the operations and I was it.

On arrival at the Centre in North Melbourne about an hour or so later, I found total chaos. Everyone was doing what they believed was necessary but the systems were totally inadequate to handle the volume of supplies and people that were appearing. The urgent tasks were to get control of the internal operations then to ensure that supplies were despatched to the areas in most need. I also needed additional help and a phone call to a colleague, Major A.O. (Tony) Purcell RAAOC, resulted in Tony coming down and, following another couple of phone calls, establishing another collection and distribution centre at the Royal Agricultural Society's Showgrounds in the suburb of Ascot Vale – a few kilometres away. Because the Showground's facility was larger and with better road transport access, Tony quickly became responsible for the bulk of the distribution process. With both locations then operational, order was established and things could proceed relatively smoothly. Within only a few hours we were despatching supplies to the areas where they were most needed.

Over the next few days we had several hundred volunteers working around the clock in both locations. Some people were accepting donations of all sorts and entering them into an inventory or providing receipts for money.

---

3   There is a very good account of the Ash Wednesday Bush Fires disaster at http://en.wikipedia. org/wiki/Ash_Wednesday_fires.

Other people were stacking and storing food and other donated items in a normal warehousing operation. A group on the phones and radio telephone was processing requests for assistance. Another group was filling orders and getting them to the despatch point, while yet another group was loading trucks and getting them away to their destinations. For about five days (the high fire intensity period), Tony and I, like other key personnel, snatched a few minutes rest when we could while the volunteers were able to be organised into three or four-hour shifts (depending on their availability) before returning to their homes and then coming back the next day to work some more.

Now the critical point in this story is that none of the several hundred people who slaved away for hours on end had received any team training for what they were doing. They were very ordinary Australians of every colour, creed and socio-economic background who heard through the radio or TV that there was a disaster and who came to give what they could – money, food, clothes, household goods, time and labour – in order to help those who were suffering. Over these days, out at the fires – which were, at that time, the worst in Australia's recorded history – in the State of Victoria alone 47 people lost their lives (including some 12 fire-fighters) and some 8,000 people were evacuated from high-risk areas. The work done by these volunteers at the State Relief Centre was crucial in terms of providing some of the help that was needed. And, in both locations, North Melbourne and the Showgrounds at Ascot Vale, people quickly fitted in and operated as cohesive teams. There was no 'team building' done; there was no worrying about interpersonal relations or any of the other myriad things that so often intrude on performance. People focused on what had to be done, asked where they could use their knowledge and skills, then set to work under intolerable conditions and for long hours simply because they knew the importance of the work. As Katzenbach and Smith found in their research, there was a real performance challenge and people rose to meet it. Teams developed, existed and worked because the challenge was real and totally understood.

My experience over the days of the Ash Wednesday Bush Fires, of course, is not news to anyone who deals with disasters – you know that people who come together for a purpose can and do function as high-performing teams despite insuperable odds simply because they are committed to doing what has to be done. And that, I suggest, is the key to any team being a success.

A 'Group' is Not a Team – So What is the Difference?

This raises the question of 'what constitutes a team?' The Oxford English Dictionary tells us that a team is: 'A group of people working or playing together' or [who] 'come together as a team to achieve something' and goes on to say it is 'a social unit that has a relatively rigid structure, organization and communication pattern. The task of each member of a team is usually well defined, and the successful functioning of the team depends on the coordinated participation of all or several members of the team.'

A clear implication from this is that simply because people have a common goal – even if they have a common pathway to that goal – they are not necessarily a team. The volunteers on Ash Wednesday had a common goal – but initially they were a disorganised group. Another simple example of this difference between a group and a team can be seen in people waiting together at a train station or a bus stop. They are all together at the one location; they all have the same goal of getting to a specific (possibly even the same) destination and they all have a common pathway to that end – the train or the bus – but they are clearly a group of individuals who just happen to be at the same spot, at the same time, with the same purpose. When I look at organisations this becomes quite an obvious similarity. It seems to me that in far too many cases the behaviour of people in so-called teams is no different from this train or bus example. All too often (and frequently because the 'leader' is in command mode rather than truly leading) people are each doing their own thing with little or no interaction or interdependence and whether or not others get to the same place at the same time is seemingly irrelevant. The only thing that is rewarded – and therefore really matters – is that 'I' achieve my goals and, again far too frequently, the means by which these goals are achieved may be of secondary importance. And this scenario is indicative of a 'group' rather than a 'team'.

The situation at the State Relief Centre in Melbourne during the Ash Wednesday Bush Fires in 1983 is an interesting example of the shift from a 'group' to a 'team'. When, quite early in the afternoon of February 16, I arrived, there were dozens of people all enthusiastically doing their own thing. There was an absolute commonality of goals – everyone wanted to help the Centre get the help needed to those facing disaster. There was some cooperation among people in places but no overall coordination with the result that people got in each other's way; the best efforts of one group unwittingly thwarting the best efforts of another group; squabbles and arguments broke out and totally unwanted bottlenecks were created everywhere. The people were 'clearly a group of individuals who just happen to be at the same spot, at the same time, with the same purpose'. My role was to bring about 'coordinated cooperation' in which the focus was on all of us reaching the same destination at the same time. My task was made very easy, first because the Chairman of the State Relief Centre, Dame Phyllis Frost, announced my arrival and role and, second, because the level of frustration being experienced brought about a situation where everyone was welcoming of some leadership. In that situation it would have been easy to slip into a command rather than a leadership role – in other words, it would have been easy to assume that, because this was only a short-term situation of a few days, people would respond to being controlled (the need of a group) rather than by encouraging innovation and creativity (the benefit of teams). Both Tony Purcell and I knew we had a narrow path on which to walk and that leadership was essential given the complexity of emotions that were involved across this volunteer force. The result of being a 'leader' rather than a 'commander' was that within about 1 and a half hours things were running smoothly and, by 6.00 pm we had supplies on their way to every affected area. The disparate groups had become high-performing teams.

I suggest that part of the reason for the pseudo teams that exist in many organisations is that, back in the 1970s and 1980s when the concept of 'teams' really took off, there was little or no real attempt to make the organisational structure changes – including remuneration and decision making – that were necessary if teams were to exist in fact as well as in theory. The result was similar to 'shifting the deck chairs on the Titanic' – on the surface things looked a bit different but nothing had really changed. We wound up with the same (or very similar) structures under different names. Unfortunately, for a lot of organisations this travesty has been allowed to continue to the present day.

Katzenbach and Smith imply that organisations exist primarily of groups and that teams may or may not exist within these groups. In studying successful teams, they found that team performance opportunities exist in all parts of the organisation in different types of work groups. They grouped these as:

- teams that recommend things (for example, task forces);

- teams that make or do things (for example, worker teams, sales teams);

- teams that run things (management teams at various levels).

This led to the realisation that teams are not often used effectively at all levels. They found that teams at the top are most difficult to form and sustain because of the complexity of long-term challenges, heavy demands on executive time and the ingrained individualism of senior people. In addition, they found that most organisations, even though they talk of teams, intrinsically prefer individual over team or group accountability. Organisations reinforce this by job descriptions, compensation systems, career paths and performance evaluations based on individuals. All these combine to legislate against the effective formation of and value of teams. In effect it leads to the 'faking' of teams in most organisations.

The price of faking a team approach either by intention or ineptitude is high. Employees resent the imposition on their time and priorities together with the diversion from their individual goals. Under the 'faking' scenario, costs can outweigh benefits, and serious animosities and distrust develop in the organisation. These undercut morale and productivity as employees see the 'team' approach as being manipulative and negative. I suggest that most of us don't need to look any further than our own organisations to see at least some evidence of this.

I suggest that a 'team' only exists when the achievement of desired results is dependent upon the interdependent efforts of every member of the team and where they all reach the desired end simultaneously. In other words, if even one team member fails to perform, there is a reduced probability of desired results being achieved but when desired results are achieved, everyone gets to the end point at the same time – and any performance rewards are shared equitably among all team members. The moment individuals are singled out for any form of reward the seeds are sown for individual performance as opposed to team performance being obtained. Sports such as basketball and football are obvious evidence of this 'reaching the end together' and it is their example that has lead to the aphorism: 'A champion team will always beat a team of champions.' Of course, getting to this position is not possible unless everyone is engaged not only with what they are doing, but also with each other and with their organisation and each person is jointly and severally fully committed to each other and their organisation.

Teams are Not Always the Answer and Why

The very fact that myriad organisations do achieve results despite the reality of 'pseudo teams' is clear evidence that teams are not always the answer.

The issue of whether or not 'teams' are needed is a human resource planning one but, because most organisations seem to work on the assumption that their existing structure is appropriate, a lot of human resource planning is largely superficial. In these instances we get back to the 'new wine into old wineskins' problem (see Chapter 2) and work groups start off with things stacked against them.

The starting question as to whether or not 'teams' are appropriate is: 'What is the minimum number of people required to achieve this result on time and within budget and what is the level of interdependence that is needed?' If achievement of results requires more than one person, this question should then be followed by ascertaining the sub-groups that may be required and, within these sub-groups, in how many will the results achieved require 'teams' – in other words, in how many sub-groups are results only possible if every person achieves what he or she is required to do – the situation in which the team can only achieve if every person achieves and every person can only achieve if the team achieves – a situation of total interdependence. You now know both where teams are necessary and how many teams are necessary. This enables you to move to the next step of putting the team together and enabling it to perform.

What I am saying is similar to the point made by Kouzes and Posner (see Chapter 6) when they argue that the first step in organisational leadership is 'to challenge the process'. Assuming that the term 'teams' can be readily and always used to describe working groups or assuming that the existing organisational structure will still be appropriate when a new strategic orientation is introduced is a recipe for failure and is always a sign that the organisation is no longer high performing no matter what its history. People quickly see through the façade of 'teams' when no team really exists or is necessary and they always recognise when they are being treated with disrespect.

Teams do Not Automatically Perform

Because, over past years, we have been seduced into using the term 'team' to describe most working groups and, as a consequence, we have operated as though any existing working group can perform effectively as a team, we have found that, in reality rather than theory, lots of 'teams' fail to perform. However, of course, as with so many other matters, most organisations refuse to let the facts get in the way of a good story. They persist as though it was the failure of the team rather than a failure of the system – the organisation and the way it is run. The result then tends to be sanctions of one sort or another against individuals who had little or no control over whether or not their 'team' could ever be really successful.

The pundits argue that, for a team to be successful, it needs to undergo a process such as 'forming, storming, norming and performing'[4] but, for success, this presupposes that there is a 'real' need for a 'team' and that the 'team' is set up for success – in other words the structure, decision-making process, rewards and so on have been examined and are being implemented in a way that is supportive of a team approach.

As was illustrated in my experience with the State Relief Centre of Victoria during the Ash Wednesday Bush Fire disaster, the movement from a disparate group of people to a high-performing team can be quite rapid. The speed with which the fires erupted and spread throughout Victoria and the fact that, at one time, the city of Melbourne (then about 2 million people) was virtually surrounded by fire so that the sound, smell and sight of the fires was readily apparent brought about a unique situation in which the whole of the State and almost every person in it was affected either directly or indirectly. According to the Victorian Government Department of Sustainability and Environment, over the five days that the fires were rampant they burned out almost 1,749 square kilometres of the State of Victoria (in other words they destroyed the equivalent of the entire State of Rhode Island in the US), destroyed around 3,000 buildings, countless native and domestic animals and farming livestock, and, of course, even more tragically took 47 lives – including those of 12 volunteer fire-fighters. Given these or similar crisis circumstances most people are highly motivated to put aside that which divides them and to concentrate on what unites them. In other words, the forming, storming, norming and performing cycle can be completed in minutes rather than hours even for quite large groups of people.

---

4   Tuckman, Bruce W. and Jensen, Mary Ann C., 'Stages of small group development revisited', *Group and Organizational Studies*, Vol. 2, 419–427.

Everyone who has been involved in dealing with emergencies can attest to this – given the combination of an obvious need, the desire to help and the opportunity to help, people will put aside other antagonisms and differences in order to focus on what is important. This is a good example of where the 'external environment' of the Leadership for Performance model (see Figure 4.1) shows itself as impacting significantly on performance in a positive way.

However, for most of us, in most situations, the situation is quite different. We are seldom in a high crisis situation. In our general working experience there are organisational goals and objectives to be attained and a dream with a date to be realised but there is no real crisis – or at least no obvious crisis or emergency about which the 'ordinary' people in the organisation are aware. Accordingly, if teams are necessary and if they are to become high performing, there is work to be done by those in leadership positions as well as those who are team members.

Developing a High-performing Team Can be Hard

Given the widespread use of 'teams', these days most people have been exposed to some form of team-building programme. These may be outdoor experiential, indoor experiential or whatever. In many instances they bring together people from disparate organisations (or disparate parts of the same organisation),give them a positive learning experience, and then encourage them to go back to their place of work and implement what has been learned.

While acknowledging that these programmes are usually very beneficial to the individual participant, in too many cases these benefits do not carry over to their organisation. The reasons for this are twofold. First, quite often every member of the participant's work group is not there at the same time and sharing the experience. Second, such exercises often concentrate on interpersonal relationships which, although important, are not the key determinants of team effectiveness.

I have referred already to the findings of Katzenbach and Smith but these ought not to be a surprise to anyone. Among other recognised key researchers on team issues are Kolb, Rubin and McIntyre. In their book *Organisational Psychology*[5] they use their research to show that effective team leaders concentrate on issues in the following order:

---

5   Kolb, David A., Rubin, Irwin M. and McIntyre, James M., *Organisational Psychology* 4th edn, Prentice Hall, New Jersey, 1984. This is also reflected in the later books by Kolb, Rubin and Osland from 1991.

- goals;

- roles;

- procedures;

- interpersonal issues.

Quite obviously, in Katzenbach and Smith's terms, making clear performance demands is synonymous with dealing with goal issues.

From my observations, the reasons for this proving successful are that such action corrects most team problems in the approximate ratio of:

- goals – 70 per cent;

- roles – 20 per cent;

- procedures – 7 per cent;

- interpersonal relationships – 3 per cent.

In other words, dealing with interpersonal relationships, important and all as they are, can never have the same positive impact as getting other issues right first. Teamwork behaviour and values such as active listening, responding constructively to the views expressed by others, dealing with controversy constructively, and supporting and recognising team members help a team perform but these values and behaviours by themselves are not exclusive to teams, nor are they sufficient to ensure team performance.

For many of us, experience bears this out. We have all seen situations where a group of people, many of whom may have 'been at each other's throats' during times when they are not frantically busy, put all that to one side in an emergency – as was obviously manifest in the achievements of the State Relief Centre of Victoria during the Ash Wednesday Bush Fires. Electricity and other utilities know that, following a natural disaster such as the cyclone that occurred in the northern suburbs of Sydney in the summer of 1991, the fires of 1994, or the widespread and devastating floods of the early 2000s, teams will work long hours with virtually no friction and achieve phenomenal results against all odds. Similarly most of us have seen situations in which groups of total strangers can come together for a relatively brief period and achieve miracles as I saw very vividly when I was leading the State Relief Centre operations during the Ash Wednesday Bushfires in Victoria. More recently in Australia, we have seen it in relation to various floods and other natural disasters as well as in the relief operations during the 2013 fires across four states, the 2001 Black Christmas Fires in NSW and in the 2009 Black Saturday Fires in Victoria. Commitment to a common goal unites and motivates.

Of course, while a demanding performance challenge (dealing with goal issues) is essential to the formation and sustenance of teams, in most cases it is not sufficient. Long-term successful teams also deal with team basics such as appropriate size, clear purpose and goals, sufficient interpersonal and group skills, a shared approach, and individual and mutual accountability.

There is yet a further aspect to consider.

Imagine trying to train footballers to work as a team by sending them on a teamwork course. Each player in turn attends the course with some cricketers, a few soccer players and a couple of tennis players. Each player attends the training and then returns to the other players to apply the knowledge gained in training. Although the individual impact of the training might be great, each of these players will need to make extra effort to transfer the training to their own environment. Worse still, the first few converts may become frustrated by their lack of team success. They may lose enthusiasm for the whole approach. Later, when larger numbers of the group have been through the course, the frustrated may even derail efforts to make the players function as a team.

We may laugh at this when it is applied to a sporting example, but how often is this exact scenario the one that is followed with business teams? Organisations need to realise that the maximum impact of working as a team can only be delivered if they work with natural work teams on their own team issues. The focus needs to be primarily on improving the ability of a specific group to function as a team. Training input on 'teams' in a theoretical framework is secondary. The group learns about teams from their own efforts to work as a team and improve their own team performance.

What all this is saying is that, if we want to develop teams, we need to realise that, as normal and natural behaviour, people, like tigers, tend to operate more as individuals than in a team. Accordingly, for many of the people we ask to operate in a team, we are asking them to perform an unnatural activity.

Is it any wonder, therefore, that teams generally work more in theory than in practice? Particularly this is the case when the leader does not have any say in selecting the team with which one is to work – which in my experience is the most common situation encountered.

In the instance where the leader is working with a 'greenfield site' then there is the opportunity to select carefully the members of the team and to ensure that everyone has such skills as complement the other team members. When this is done properly then it is possible to quickly develop an effective and efficient team. There are many good tools that are readily available to assist in the recruitment of teams in any situation and they are particularly useful in a 'greenfield' situation. Two tools that I have found very powerful are the DISC[6] and Myers Briggs[7] instruments. Unfortunately we seldom have the opportunity to work with a 'greenfield site' and, even when we do, we generally fail to handle the situation correctly. However both DISC and Myers Briggs (among others) profiles can be powerful aids in helping leaders in the development of existing teams.

Following Kolb, Rubin and McIntyre's work (as well as Katzenbach and Smith's), the steps to develop teams are to deal in order with:

- goal issues;

- role issues;

- procedural issues;

- interpersonal issues.

The type and quality of immediate leadership provided is crucial for teams that have a high probability of become high performing. Right at the start it is important that the team leader concentrates on focusing the team, defining goals, roles and responsibilities. This ensures everyone clearly understands what has to be done and it instils a sense of purpose among team members. During this first phase, communication is primarily one-way, from team leader to team members as the parameters within which the team will operate are set.

---

6   The DISC profile material is available from many sources and there is a good discussion on it at http://en.wikipedia.org/wiki/DISC_assessment.
7   Information about the Myers Briggs material is available at http://www.myersbriggs.org/my-mbti-personality-type/mbti-basics/.

As the team members buy in to their responsibilities and start to understand their accountabilities, the leader needs to ensure that he or she both invites and responds appropriately to questions. Here the team leader clarifies team activities and fine tunes roles and responsibilities. Clearly communication is now becomes more multi-way between team leader and team members.

As the team starts to harmonise together, the role of the team leader moves to facilitating self-direction. Here the team leader involves the team in setting its own goals and directions – something most teams are very happy with once they know what they need to achieve and the parameters within which they can operate. Once this stage is reached, in many ways the role of the team leader is best filled by the team leader acting as an active team member – one among equals. This can then lead to the situation where the team becomes virtually autonomous and highly effective – the only role the immediate leader now needs to have is to act as a conduit to the rest of the organisation.

As was stated at the outset of this chapter, the catchword has become 'teams'. There is a very good reason for this. Teams do work. Teams are a good idea. Teams can produce everything that the theories claim they will. Team leadership means dealing with all the appropriate issues so that the theory can be seen in practice. However for this to happen, we need to take account of the issues raised above but we also need to take account of the fact that there can still be some additional difficulties that will emerge – and these can lead us to 'death valley'.

There is a 'Death Valley' with Teams

Experience indicates that despite the best team member selection and the best intentions of everyone involved, and despite training using the best programmes, invariably teams go through a predictable cycle in terms of performance. My observations of a very common cycle found among teams are illustrated in Figure 4.1.

This curve illustrates the progress of a group of people through the 'pseudo-team' stage in which enthusiasm and good intentions sometimes substitute for performance, through the development of a way in which everyone can work together, to the final stage where the team is a high performing one. Unfortunately, from my observations, too often insufficient attention is paid to this process with the result that inadequate time is allowed for the development

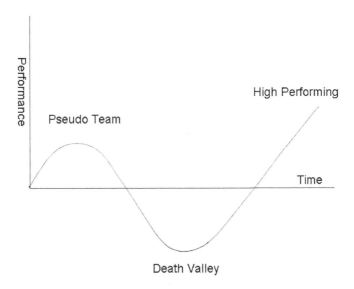

Figure 4.1   The team performance curve

process, scant attention is paid to possible regression should there be any changes in team membership or performance parameters, and the 'team' sometimes degenerates into a bunch of individuals doing what they believe is required regardless of the impact on the team overall. This is 'death valley'. When this happens, results may be achieved – even the desired results – but this has occurred *despite* the 'team' rather than *because of* the 'team'.

I call this degenerative stage 'death valley'. In my experience, quite soon after a team comes together and after initial successes have been achieved, there can come a 'down' period. It is almost as though, at the start of the team experience, an enthusiasm (which can sometimes lead to complacency) sets in – a 'hooray, this is working, aren't we great', sort of mentality develops. This is caused, in part, by relief (or hope) that this present experience is not going to reproduce past experience of teams that were less than successful. I call this the 'pseudo team' stage because although results start being seen, they are not necessarily sustainable – and sustainability is something that is essential if the team is to be operating effectively over protracted periods.

In teams that come together for short, highly focused purposes such as dealing with emergencies – the Ash Wednesday Bush Fires sort of scenario – this move through a 'pseudo team' either never emerges or, if it does, is not too much of a problem. But in organisations where 'teams' seem to be expected to function for prolonged periods it can be a very real concern. It is at this point that the role of the leader is particularly important to refocus the team on their goals and to provide socio-emotional support as required. Unless the leader is alert to this 'death valley' probability there is a very real danger that the team will disintegrate and the remnant will be an on-going, marginally effective pseudo team that will probably impact negatively on the achievement of a high-performing organisation. To move the team out of 'death valley' the team leader will need to refocus his or her team and he or she will probably find that this is the time when attention needs to be paid to the 'procedures' and 'interpersonal relationships' factors of which Kolb Rubin and McIntyre spoke.

In order to help a team through this stage, a team leader will find cognitive coaching a powerful tool – but always remember that the effectiveness of this cognitive coaching can be highly dependent upon the extent to which the executive have developed or are developing a coaching and mentoring culture throughout the organisation because this appropriate culture is an extremely important consideration if teams are to operate effectively.

Chapter Summary

This chapter has explored the issue of teams in developing and maintaining a high-performing organisation. It has stressed that:

- The concept of teams is very often abused as organisations use this concept to describe their traditional organisational structure under different terminology. The result is that most 'teams' perform at a far lower level than is desired or even possible.

- Teams can be (and should be) a critical aspect of every organisation because they contain many of the seeds for high performance.

- For teams to perform as they should, organisations need to create an environment in which the probability of success is high and this requires both examining the real need for a team then, if a team is required, understanding the dynamics involved and providing whole-of-team development.

- There is a wide range of very effective team-building programmes and processes available but an organisation should be careful to select those that are compatible with its desired culture.

- Coaching and mentoring are essential parts of the process to obtaining a high-performing team.

Taking the Fourth Step to a High-performing Organisation

Consider your own organisation – the one in which you work:

- To what extent is the term 'teams' used as a generic description of working groups or units?

- What is the process used to determine whether or not 'teams' are the appropriate work unit for any area or project?

- To what extent does your organisation consider the type of teams that might be required or appropriate and then carefully select the members of each of these teams?

- What is the process used to develop 'teams' in your organisation and how effective is this? How could this process be improved?

- What are the things in your organisation that work against or prevent teams being as effective as they could or should be?

- How can these be corrected?

5

Individual Performance

Time and again when I discuss performance issues with executives, it is the performance of the individuals at the lower levels of the organisation on which they focus. I have lost count of the number of times executives have clearly assumed (or stated) that their own performance is fine but that their organisation is suffering because of the quality and quantity of work done by other people. As the Vision into Action process makes clear, until and unless all of the earlier issues at board and executive level are fully attended to, it is unrealistic to expect high performance from your staff. In other words, be very careful about pointing at others until your own performance is fully in order.

The winter 1993 edition of *Sloan Management Review* contained an article entitled 'How Can Organisations Learn Faster? The Challenge of Entering the Green Room'.[1] In this the author, Edgar H. Schein, argues that it is not enough for an organisation to know where it wants to go or even to reward people for moving in the desired direction. He argues that the past experience of failure or punishment holds people back and must be dealt with. He calls this situation Anxiety 1 and shows how it stops people from taking actions that would move them out of where they feel comfortable. Schein argues that to deal with this we need to create what he calls Anxiety 2. Anxiety 2 arises when people realise that the risk of not moving is greater than the risk of staying where one is now. The challenge is, he says, to walk the thin line between creating a fear of not moving and a fear that immobilises. Anxiety 2 is the fear, shame or guilt associated with not learning anything new.

Schein argues that organisations will not achieve their strategic directions – realise their vision – unless an appropriate mechanism is introduced to manage these two anxieties and the gulf between them. Today we know that Schein was half right – fear of failure certainly holds people back as does past experience

---

1   Schein, Edgar H., 'How Can Organisations Learn Faster? The Challenge Of Entering the Green Room', *Sloan Management Review*, Winter 1993.

of how things work and it is difficult to walk the thin line between creating a fear of not moving and a fear that immobilises. But now we also know that it is absence of fear that is necessary if people are to move forward. In other words, rather than a need to engender Schein's Anxiety 2, we need to bring about a culture in which people feel physically and emotionally safe and where they know that failure when attempting the new will not be used as a cause for punishment but rather as an opportunity for learning. This is only possible when there is an environment in which people at all levels are fully engaged with and committed to their work, their work group and the organisation itself.

Schein's article leads to the whole question of people management including such topics as 'Are your people an expense or an investment?' and 'What is the role that human resource development should play in maintaining and developing the value of your investment in people?'

In most traditional organisations a significant proportion of the on-going costs relate to staff – inclusive of the board and executive team. This is why, when the time comes for cost-cutting, attention invariably goes to reducing staff numbers (usually at lower staff levels), minimising or removing salary increases (unfortunately, in many organisations, this also is seen as appropriate only for lower level staff), raising the bar for payment of bonuses (again at least for lower-level staff), and the like. In other words, despite the rhetoric that 'we invest in people', most organisations seem to see their people (other than the executives) as an expense that can be reduced almost on the whim of top management. While, at least in theory, those at the top of an organisation will argue that reducing these costs will result in better profits being available to shareholders, in most cases the fact remains that they recognise that reducing these costs heightens the probability that their own bonus entitlements will be preserved. This, unfortunately, is one of the totally predictable side effects of the understandably short-term focus that permeates the board and executive teams of most organisations today. (You might want to refer back to Chapter 2 where I refer to the *McKinsey Review* article 'Encouraging your people to take the long view').[2]

The compulsory reduction of staff levels is always expensive not only because of the immediate monetary outlay but, in the long term often more important, its impact on the image of the organisation and its 'good will' – if you like, the 'collateral damage'. The everyday operating costs of staff turnover

---

2   http://www.mckinseyquarterly.com/Retail_Consumer_Goods/Strategy_Analysis/
    Encouraging_your_people_to_take_the_long_view_3014, September 2012.

is itself expensive yet often this is ignored because it is seldom calculated. (I define labour turnover as 'a separation for any reason followed by the intention to immediately replace' because this definition ensures that increases in staffing levels because of organisational growth or reductions in staffing levels because of organisational decline are not included in turnover figures. In addition this definition also allows for meaningful comparisons across time periods and organisations.) My studies indicate that, using this definition, the costs to any organisation are not less than a multiple of 500 for the hourly rate of any person replaced and that the more senior the person being replaced, the higher the multiplier. But this cost can pall into insignificance compared with the long-term negative image effect experienced by any organisation that goes through reasonable frequent (say five to ten years) cycles of retrenchments, redundancies and the like. Today many organisations claim that they are or that they want to be 'employers of choice' but organisations that develop a history of 'downsizing' or 'rightsizing' at reasonably frequent intervals have a very hard job of actually becoming an 'employer of choice' – or of being seen as 'high performing'!

As I say, this issue of staff turnover is an important one that often fails to receive the attention it warrants. Far too often organisations consider the costs only in relation to advertising and any fees that may be paid to any consultancy. But the costs are far more than that. For example, a prestige car dealership struggles to run its service department at the optimum number of service jobs per day at a time when its competitor dealerships in the same franchise are doing very well with their service departments fully booked week in and week out. This particular dealership has some of the best qualified and most competent service technicians available – all fully trained by the prestige brand the dealership represents – yet this major profit source ('service' is one of two major profit sources in most automotive dealerships – the other one is 'parts') struggles to make budget. When followed up in customer satisfaction surveys, it is clear that customers are very happy with the quality of service yet they often go elsewhere. Why? According to the customers when independently surveyed it's because of an issue relating to the service advisors – those people who first meet you when you take your car in for service and who organise the service for you. At this dealership they're never the same and they vary a lot in their competence. The dealership in question has trouble keeping its service advisors and service technicians with the result that customers cannot develop any form of relationship with the dealership through one known contact. The turnover of service advisors and service technicians, while relatively inexpensive in terms of advertising and other fees, is actually costing this dealership hundreds of thousands of dollars in revenue and they appear totally unable or unwilling to recognise this fact and deal with it by replacing the service manager – a man who is widely seen (by the service technicians and the service advisors) as being toxic and who actively dissuades service advisors from giving customers the full story as to what needs to be done to their vehicle and what charges will be involved (which leads to a selling on price approach). Senior management find it easier to blame the service advisors and service technicians for customer disenchantment because these are relatively easy to replace. In this company (as in so many others), no-one from top management is prepared to confront the real issue.

While it is true that many organisations require employees to complete employment contracts and invariably these contracts have some form of 'do not compete' clauses to cover the issue of 'poaching' should that employee leave for any reason, no such contract can cover every contingency. What is the real cost to an accounting, consulting, legal or similar professional practice when a senior employee or partner leaves (or is dismissed) and, of their own volition, clients of the original practice find out where this person has gone and they then choose to take their business to the new operation? Is it really possible (or even economically feasible) to take legal action seeking damages? What sum would be claimed? What are the chances of any legal action being successful if the person involved can prove they didn't either advertise their leaving or approach their original employer's clients but that these clients came across because they valued a particular personal relationship? And if the legal action was successful, would those clients then return to your fold or would they go to some third party as a sign of their disgust with your actions?

Similarly, what is the cost of a successful salesperson changing jobs? In this world where 'price' is so often the selling determinant does 'brand loyalty' really exist to any great extent or is repeat business rather because of loyalty to a particular salesperson who is known and trusted? What is the real cost to a manufacturing organisation when experienced factory staff leave and new people have to be recruited and trained? How long does it take to instil in these new people that 'sixth sense' or 'feeling' that enabled previous staff members to know, almost intuitively, when something was wrong – and how to fix it? What is the cost of the loss of a clerk who has had long and friendly contact with suppliers and customers and who can draw on this when necessary to get orders expedited and/or smooth troubled waters caused by non-delivery, late delivery or other customer-related problems? All these 'extra' (and often unrecognised) costs are still part of the true cost of labour turnover.

I could provide examples from myriad other industries and organisations, but the key message is that your labour turnover is probably costing you far more than you realise – and it could send you broke!

High-performing organisations are able to become 'employers of choice' partly because the way they are seen to deal with staff and with staffing issues helps them to maintain a highly positive public image. A high labour turnover can destroy this quest and provide a totally different image. In this section we discuss ways that can help organisations on this quest to be 'employers of choice' – a key indicator of a high-performing organisation.

Capability

The first step is to revisit the concept of capability.

Capability is the extent to which an individual or organisation is able to do certain things. In an individual it is a combination of a person's knowledge, ability or 'competence' and their confidence, motivation or 'willingness' to perform certain tasks or activities.

Organisations select employees on the basis of their implied capability – in other words, the recruitment and interviewing process is (or should be) designed to ascertain that a person has the requisite knowledge, qualifications and experience for the vacancy and that there is a cultural fit between the organisation and the prospective employee. This is why focusing on verifiable evidence of what a person has achieved is so important. But this process, even if complemented with the very best psychometric testing, cannot always determine whether or not a person will actually prove to have the capability required. Only time on the job will show this. As most employers know, a failure to demonstrate the necessary level of capability is a key reason why so many people leave (or are asked to leave) an organisation within 12 months of being appointed to a new role.

From my arguments in the earlier chapters it should be clear that, when the Vision into Action process is followed, the determination of what capability an organisation needs, what capability it already has and any gaps should become apparent at least by the time the 'teams-goals' level in the process has been reached. This capability factor is supportive, of course, of the Leadership for Performance model's assertion that dealing with the people issues (human process) should be the last step in creating an environment in which people have a high probability of achieving success. The importance of this human process factor is one important reason why I believe that the most senior HR person in any organisation should always be a member of the senior executive and have the same status as every other senior executive.

The step to determining requisite capability starts with the dream with a date – what resources are required by the organisation in order to bring the vision into medium-term reality?

In most cases this then leads to at least one of the objectives dealing with issues of resources but in this, 'resources' must also deal with such matters as the number of people who will be employed at the finite date prescribed and the skills, knowledge and experience that they will need to demonstrate in order for the organisation to be successful. Of course, such an approach doesn't necessarily mean that the organisation will be expanding – it could just as easily mean that greater productivity is to be achieved with personnel numbers remaining static and/or that the organisation is downsizing for some or another reason. In one organisation with which I was involved this approach showed that there would be some 1,500 less employees within five years and opened discussion as to how this could be done in the most positive possible way for those affected. In another organisation where the Vision into Action process was used to close an operation following a takeover, the fact that the business was closing was made very clear. This information was made public and was used to work with people and any unions affected as to the 'how' this could be achieved in the most positive manner.

Understandably the organisation's strategic orientation as agreed with the executive and board will also impact on this capability question – almost always an organisation with the strategic orientation of being driven by customers'/clients' needs and satisfaction will require higher staff levels than will an organisation driven by some internal orientation. This assessment of requisite capability will then flow down through determination around teams and, eventually, to the people who are to be employed and to the terms under which they are to be employed.

Recruitment and Induction

Ultimately recruitment and induction are the responsibility of line management. The HR Department may act as a facilitator in this process, but it is line management who must take responsibility (and accountability) for the final recruitment decision and for the actual induction of the appointee into their new role.

RECRUITMENT

Whether the recruitment is for a new position or to replace an existing person, the first stage is to determine exactly what the person will be doing and that for which he or she will be responsible. This means that the appropriate position description should be developed or fully revised prior to any recruitment process being commenced – in an ideal situation, the current incumbent should be involved in this revision as, almost invariably, there are practical changes that occur over the duration of any incumbency – even a relatively short one. The recruitment process can then focus both on what the new appointee will actually be doing when they take up their appointment and on any further activities that are likely to be required of the appointee within the short to medium term.

The second stage in any recruitment process is to develop a profile of the person needed – what qualifications and experience are critical if the appointee is to have a high probability of success. It is important that these be realistic. One of the difficulties often encountered is that 'wish lists' become substituted for 'vitals' with the result that the best person for the position (that is, the person who best matches the profile) may be overlooked or may not even bother to apply. A properly constructed profile enables a precise check list to be prepared against which all applicants can be assessed – such a process reduces the probability of bias, nepotism and/or discrimination for any reason whatever.

The third stage, of course, is making the vacancy known. Obviously a recruitment consultancy can be used or the organisation can do the job themselves. There are many avenues for advertising a vacancy today and the wise organisation utilises a variety of these – including trade or professional magazines and/or educational institutions for specialist positions. The important thing is that whatever avenue (or avenues) is used, the advertisement provides factual information and clear guidelines for prospective applicants.

Organisations that 'gild the lily' about the position or its prospects quickly lose credibility while organisations who fail to be clear as to the sort of person they are seeking may find much time is wasted in sifting through applications that are totally inappropriate and which, with a better-worded advertisement, may not have been made.

When the organisation is doing its own recruitment, if the check list has been properly and adequately prepared then the first culling of applications can be done either by a computer programme or a junior staff member – after all, this first stage is a basically clerical task to eliminate any application that does not meet the minimum defined criteria. Of course, if such culling cannot be done almost automatically then there's probably something wrong with your person specification and this specification problem has spilled over into the check list which you developed from it.

An important issue here is the acknowledgment of applications which, ideally, should be done immediately an application is received. This acknowledgement should let the applicant know the date by which a decision will be made and how the applicant will be notified of the outcome. Whether or not an applicant is successful, all applicants will form an opinion of your organisation by the response they get either directly from you or, if a consultancy is used, indirectly from you. If you are a frequent user of a particular consultancy or if you are a relatively frequent advertiser for staff, this can be important. You, or the consultancy you use, is either increasing or decreasing that intangible known as 'good will' by the way in which applicants are treated. Unfortunately many consultancies and quite a few employing organisations seem to forget this – they are so swamped with applications of one sort or another that they forget or ignore the common courtesy of acknowledgement even though with today's technology this can be done so easily and quickly via an automated response.

Following the initial culling to remove patently unsuitable candidates, a more detailed perusal of the remaining applications is required. By definition, those remaining after the initial cull are all potentially suitable because they have met the essential criteria. What you are now doing is grading the remainder in accord with their overall suitability. The purpose of this is to decide who, if any, should be advanced to interview stage. You probably don't want to interview every potentially suitable applicant but you certainly want to interview the apparently most suitable applicants. Interviews, done properly, are time consuming and relatively stressful for everyone involved. You want to interview enough people in order to have a choice, but not so many people that your decision-making process becomes overloaded. From my experience both as a manager and as an employer, interviewing around three to five people is about right.

There is a trap here into which many organisations fall. That is the trap of 'desperation' that occurs when none of the applicants really fits your criteria yet the pressure is on to fill the post. The danger is that you will proceed with someone who is far less than ideal for the vacancy – and that is an activity that is fraught with further danger down the track. As a general rule, for a potentially high-performing organisation it is usually better for the vacancy to remain than for you to fill it with the wrong person – and interviewing people despite them either not meeting or only marginally meeting essential criteria can lead to this mistake.

Now comes the interview. There are two commonly encountered problems in relation to interviews – inadequate preparation and insufficient time. Both of these are usually caused because of other work pressures and an apparently underlying belief that, because of general knowledge and experience, 'it won't take long' and 'I know how to interview'! Both of which are very often wrong!

I have learned to allocate at least one and a half hours for each interview so that I have time to refresh my memory before the interview, conduct an interview for about an hour, then write up my thoughts after the interview. I have also learned to have a set of prepared questions that I will use for every person to ensure that I cover the same ground with each of them. These questions will focus on their experience for the position under consideration either in terms of 'tell me about when …' or 'what would you do if …' My emphasis is to concentrate on things that are job-related. Naturally any question which could lead to even the slightest thought or suggestion of discrimination is totally avoided – this is especially important in locations or positions where legislation allows disaffected applicants to appeal and requires that all appellants are given access to all the interviewers' notes.

The sorts of questions I find useful are shown in the below example (which are not original but for which I am unable to locate the source). Although I am not a recruitment specialist, I am often asked to sit on selection committees and I have used these (or questions based on them) for a wide range of management and technical positions across a broad spectrum of organisations in various countries.

Interview Questions

1. Tell me about yourself?

2. What are you looking for in a role?

3. What made you apply for this particular position? What interested you the most/least about it?

Organisational fit

4. Can you tell me in which of the following areas in your previous positions you enjoyed the most/least and why?

Technical and professional knowledge

5. Sometimes it's easy to get in 'over your head'. Describe a situation where you had to request help or assistance on a project or assignment?

Teamwork

6. Give me an example of when you worked as a member of a team. What was your contribution to that team?

7. Describe a situation in which you found that your results were not up to your manager's expectations. What happened? What action did you take?

Analysis

8. We can sometimes identify a small problem and fix it before it becomes a major problem. Give an example of how you have done this.

9. Recall a time when you were assigned what you considered to be a complex project. Specifically, what steps did you take to prepare for and finish the project? Were you happy with the outcome? What one step would you have done differently if given the chance?

Adaptability

10.   Tell me of some situations in which you have had to adjust quickly to changes over which you had no control. What was the impact of the change on you?

Work standards

11.   Describe a time when you were not very satisfied or pleased with your performance. What did you do about it?

Job motivation

12.   What kind of manager do you work best for? Provide examples.

Initiative

13.   Can you give us an example of an achievement and what was the result?

14.   Describe a situation that required a number of things to be done at the same time. How did you handle it? What was the result?

Ability to learn/self-development

15.   What steps have you taken to improve your own skills?

16.   What techniques have you learnt to make yourself more effective in your job? How did you learn them?

Professionalism

17.   Tell me about how you handled a situation where you had to follow a directive that you didn't necessarily agree with and what happened?

Ability to cope with pressure

18.   What was the most stressful time you have ever had in a role?

Planning and organising

19.   How do you determine priorities in scheduling your time? Give examples.

Communication

20.   Tell me of a time when your active listening skills really paid off for you – maybe a time when other people missed the key idea being expressed.

Customer orientation

21.   Tell me of the most difficult customer service experience that you have ever had to handle. Can you be specific and tell me what you did and what was the outcome.

Work ethic

22.   How would you describe your work ethic? Can you give me an example that demonstrates this?

What these questions are seeking to ascertain is the suitability of a candidate for a particular position as well as getting an indication of how well they may fit with the organisation's culture.

Culture fit is extremely important in recruitment. My research shows that when most people join an organisation, they do so because they believe that there is a reasonable degree of compatibility between their values and behaviours and those of the organisation. This is an aspect of 'culture'. Invariably there is some amount of gap that becomes apparent once the employment commences but, in most cases, this gap is sufficiently small for it not to be an issue. In some instances, however, it quickly becomes obvious that the gap is larger than was originally thought and, unless the new employee is prepared to make some significant changes in attitude and/or behaviour, a separation is imminent. Support for my research about the importance of culture fit came in December 2012 when Professor Lauren Rivera[3] of Northwestern University's School of Management presented research showing that top-performing firms in the US

3   'Hiring as Cultural Matching: The Case of Elite Professional Service Firms', *American Sociological Review*, Vol. 77, No. 6, 999–1022, December 2012.

recruited people who were culturally similar in terms of interests, experiences and personal presentation. The emphasis of these firms was stated to be on cultural fit as critical to employment decisions. My research shows that most of the separations – whether initiated by the individual or the organisation – that occur within the first 12 months can, at least in part, be sheeted home to this issue of culture fit. Of course there are also separations because of misleading information being given by either (or both) parties and other reasons but cultural fit was most prominent. And, as I have said, such turnover is not only annoying – it is expensive.

A tool that can be very useful in terms of this culture fit is psychometric testing. A good psychologist, using appropriate instruments, can be a wonderful help in providing information that will either confirm initial impressions from the resume and interview, or will raise questions that necessitate further investigation. The effectiveness of psychometric testing partly depends on the quality of interpretation done by the psychologist but, even when the very best psychologist is used, it is not infallible and, to my mind, it does not replace interviews. However I like to use psychometric testing as it can be a powerful adjunct to interviews because, as I said, it can confirm earlier impressions from the interview or can raise new questions that will then need to be addressed.

Culture fit is always a key component of recruitment in high-performing organisations and, for some, it is *the* key selection criterion.

One further note before moving from the interview stage. Although most people are basically honest, as most recruiters know, there can be a temptation to stretch the truth and sometimes this extends to qualifications. I always request original documents to be brought to any interview (no, I don't like 'certified copies' – I've been caught out by these!) and, when I have still had my suspicions, I then check with public documentation from the nominated institution – most institutions have graduation lists, yearbooks or the like that can be accessed quite readily and with no breach of confidentiality (although this will generally give only a name and people have been known to steal identities).

The final stage in deciding who to employ is the checking of references. Even when written references have been supplied, I still seek verbal references as sometimes it is not so much what is said but the way in which it is said as well as what is *not* said that gives the most information. This can be a delicate area and some organisations have a blanket ban on confirming anything other than a person's employment record. Where possible I seek to speak with an applicant's past managers or supervisors and I concentrate on ascertaining facts rather than opinions. The answers to some of the questions I have shown above are useful in framing the questions I put to referees but care must be taken to avoid 'leading questions' in which there is an implied 'right' answer. My final question to all referees is always 'I understand that this is hypothetical, but if xxx applied to join you again either where you are now or in a future position, would you re-employ him or her?' No matter what the reply, sometimes a very, very long pause between the question and response can be very instructive!

The recruitment phase then concludes with notifying all unsuccessful applicants as to the result. Again, many organisations fail to do this – a sign of discourtesy that can have an impact on the way the organisation or its consultancy is later viewed by many people. In these days of emails, notifying unsuccessful applicants in a timely and courteous fashion takes very little time while quietly promoting an organisation's image as one that is genuinely interested in people.

A final point before we leave recruitment and selection. Always remember that the best applicants will have their own alternatives. If a person is actively seeking another position they are probably applying to more than one organisation. The good applicants are likely to have more offers than just yours and they will be weighing up the pros and cons of each of these. When you have finished your interviewing and decided who you want to employ, act promptly. I have seen too many organisations fail to get the person they really want because their internal decision-making process is too slow, inadequate and unduly convoluted.

INDUCTION

This is the first part of setting a person up for success in their new appointment. It doesn't matter how big or how small the organisation, there is always some paper work or other administrative function to be completed, some policies and practices to be explained and some people to meet. Whether done on a one-with-one basis or, if there are several people commencing on the same day, in a group, the material that needs to be covered right at the outset of employment should include most, if not all, of that shown in Table 5.1.

Table.5.1   General induction

i.   Explaining the history, vision, mission, functions and organisation of the organisation.

ii.   Working hours and company rules and regulations including usage of alcohol, drugs, bullying, discrimination and so on, policies and practices.

iii.   Holidays, sick leave, other leave entitlements and policies.

iv.   Salary, schedule and administration and salary reviews.

v.   Fringe benefits and other perquisites.

vi.   Grievance procedures.

vii.   IT usage including email policies and practice.

viii.   Telephone/social networking policies.

ix.   Professionalism in the organisation.

x.   Conflicts of interest.

xi.   Privacy.

xii.   Security issues.

xiii.   Petty cash.

xiv.   All HR policies including EEO, OH&S, personal and professional development, and dismissal.

xv.   Performance appraisal system.

xvi.   Recapping of the terms and conditions pertaining to 'probationary period of employment'.

This should be done by the person responsible for HR issues immediately the person commences employment and I do not believe there are many (if any) legitimate excuses for not completing it within the first day.

When this induction is completed, the new employee should be escorted to their work area and their immediate manager or supervisor should then complete job-specific induction which could include the topics in Table 5.2. The reason for this is that, no matter how qualified and experienced a new employee may be, every organisation (and sometimes every manager) has its own ways of doing things and it is important that these organisation-specific practices are known and understood.

Table 5.2   Job-specific induction

i.   Introduction of the new employee to all people with whom he or she will come in contact on the job. This should be done by physically taking the new employee around at least the work-specific area and introducing them but should include visits to others where appropriate.

ii.   Explaining all aspects of the work station – including use of appropriate electronic and physical filing systems and all aspects of the IT system as they apply to the new employee. This includes explaining all aspects of renewal of supplies including ordering of stationery and so on.

iii.   Special requirements as to departmental practices.

iv.   Setting up the systems and procedures that will be used to provide training and coaching as well as performance assessment during the probationary period of employment.

I know that this is time consuming and can be seen as quite onerous – another good reason for controlled labour turnover – but high-performing organisations understand its importance and they ensure both that adequate time is available and that the whole process is done well. In fact, in most high-performing organisations, this matter of effective recruitment and induction becomes one of the criteria – a KPI – by which a leader's performance is assessed.

Training, Education or Development?

In almost all cases people have some need for further development – even at executive level (even though far too few executives will openly or readily acknowledge this). Some years ago I read an article that argued, no matter how qualified a person might be or what their experience is, they need to update their expertise at least every five years – this 'five-year' period was labelled the 'half-life' of managerial knowledge and competence. The article also pointed out that this need for development is generally ignored by people at the higher organisational echelons even though, given their responsibility, their need is probably the greatest. Today many organisations can get into trouble because their people, right across the organisational spectrum, are using yesterday's approaches to deal with tomorrow's problems!

Professor Leonard Nadler of George Washington University argues that part of the reason for failure to properly benefit from human resource development is that organisations fail to understand the complexity of the human resource development function. Nadler[4] argues that there is a distinction between training, education and development (see Table 5.3) and that it is only when this distinction is understood that appropriate evaluation of human resource development outcomes is possible.

Table 5.3   The distinction between human resource development activities

Activity	Focus	Time Utilisation	Financial Resource	Risk Level
Training	Present Job	Now	Expense	Low
Education	Future Job	Soon	Investment – Short Term	Medium
Development	Organisation	Sometime	Investment – Long Term	High

---

4   Nadler, Leonard, *Corporate Human Resources Development: A Management Tool*, Van Nostrand Company, New York, 1980.

What Nadler is saying is that, for optimum results from human resource development activities, an organisation needs to know whether they are enabling someone to do their present job more effectively, preparing them for their next job or providing information that they *may* need in the future. He points out that, no matter the economic and other pressures, there is almost always some need for some training which should show its benefits almost immediately whereas education and development tend to be discretionary endeavours from which benefits can become apparent only after considerable time has elapsed and from which, because circumstances change over time, the anticipated benefits may not ever be realised.

This distinction is understood and applied by high-performing organisations and, as a direct consequence, they spend time with every employee – especially new appointees – to ascertain and attend to training needs while flagging both educational and developmental needs for future attention.

In high-performing organisations there is another important element to this human resource development activity. This is the extent to which people receive support when they are on various programmes. For effective Human Resource Development (HRD) intervention the active support of participants' managers is critical. This support should include:

1.   Preparing participants for the coming programme by making very clear the expectations held by their manager.

2.   Supporting participants during their training by ensuring their jobs are 'covered' and that participants are not trying to do their normal work simultaneously with workshop participation.

3.   Facilitating application of learning back into the workplace by coaching and support.

A clear understanding of these issues then enables appropriate evaluation of all human resource development activities. It is important that neither the provider of the HRD intervention nor those undergoing human resource development activities are assessed by generally inappropriate criteria such as the normal 'evaluation sheet' that is invariably completed at the close of a programme. No matter what the programme-end evaluation sheet may say, if a training intervention results in improved performance back on the job, the intervention has done what it is supposed to do. Similarly, if an education or development activity results in no appreciable immediate improvement back on the job it doesn't mean the intervention was unsuccessful as its impact was never designed to be 'immediate'. And, along with these, any evaluation of any intervention needs to take account of the degree of support provided before, during and after the intervention activity. If the appropriate support has not been provided then the organisation – not the participant or provider – is also (and possibly primarily) at fault.

High-performing organisations know this.

Performance Appraisal

One of the most commonly encountered activities in all organisations today is that of performance appraisal. In my experience this is an activity that seldom operates as it should and to which, far too frequently, there is more verbal assent rather than effective implementation. As *Fortune Magazine*[5] once pointed out, most managers hate conducting performance appraisals and if they think they can get away with not doing them or, at best, doing them in only a perfunctory manner, they will. However, in high-performing organisations, performance appraisals are a vital part of their *modus operandi*.

The concept of performance appraisals (both formal and informal or structured and unstructured) has been around for a long time. Back in 1957 Douglas McGregor, the author of *The Human Side of Enterprise*, said of performance appraisal processes:[6]

> *Formal performance appraisal plans are designed to meet three needs, one for the organization and two for the individual:*
>
> - *They provide systematic judgements to back up salary increases, promotions, transfers, and sometimes demotions and terminations.*
> - *They are a means of telling a subordinate how he is doing, and suggesting needed changes in his behaviour, attitudes, skills or job knowledge; they let him know 'where he stands' with the boss.*

---

5   'How to Appraise Performance', *Fortune Magazine*, October 12, 1987.
6   McGregor, Douglas, 'An Uneasy Look at Performance', *Harvard Business Review*, May–June, 1957.

- *They are also being increasingly used as a basis for the coaching and counselling of the individual by the superior.*

These purposes are still valid – in fact it could be argued that they have even more relevance today than ever before. However the way in which they are achieved needs to be reconsidered and, as high-performing organisations know, probably revamped.

In the current ideal world, the performance appraisal process starts with the organisation's vision, mission, values, dream with a date, strategies and objectives. These elements set the framework for determining KRAs and KPIs against which everyone in the organisation is assessed. What this means is that, for example, if a core strategic orientation is 'focus on the customer' then a KRA will be 'customer service' and a KPI will consider both the quality and quantity of such service provided by people at each organisational level. This KPI measure will be directly related to the organisation's objectives and dream with a date.

There are some difficulties with this approach. The first difficulty is that this approach is driven from the top of the organisation – it is 'top-down' – and, particularly at the lower organisational levels, it can be seen as having very little to do with the reality under which they work. The second difficulty is that this approach can degenerate into acting as though the organisation is operating in a closed system (see Chapter 1) and, as such, it fails to give appropriate consideration to both the quantitative (hard measures) and qualitative (descriptive measures) factors relating to performance. Also, although many of these performance appraisals operate as the end result of '360' appraisals, in reality most weight tends to be given to the opinion held by the person's immediate manager – and he or she is usually the person conducting the appraisal. A scepticism can (and often does) develop in which individuals feel that it doesn't matter what they or others may say, only the manager's opinion will really receive attention.

What if there was an alternative approach – an approach that encouraged everyone to be fully engaged with the performance appraisal process and with which they felt fully involved? What if a performance appraisal process accepted the importance and validity of the organisation's vision, mission, values, dream with a date, objectives and strategies but then developed the performance appraisal process in a different way?

There is a different approach – and many high-performing organisations both know it and use it!

At every level in every organisation there are people affected by the outputs of what other people do. For example, external customers and clients are affected by the manner in which those having direct customer contact interact with them (and that includes functions such as the invoicing and related functions in accounts); front-line staff are affected by the manner with which their supervisors and managers interact with them, managers are affected by the manner with which executives interact with them. What I am suggesting is that, across the board, all 'internal customers' are affected by the manner with which their 'suppliers' interact with them. Working from this premise a different approach to performance appraisal has been developed and implemented and this has received very high levels of acceptance and support across the organisations where it is used. This different approach is one in which the starting point is the people affected by what other people do.

In this approach – a 'bottom-up' approach – 'customers' (both the external and internal people affected by what other people do) are asked to define their ideal supplier and/or customer. (Some people are both 'customer' and 'supplier'. For example, a person's supervisor or manager is probably both of these as an individual will receive instructions and so on from their leader as well as providing their leader with performance output.) From the list that develops from the responses of all customers and all suppliers, factor analysis is used to ascertain the critical elements and a performance appraisal questionnaire is developed from these. Now, when it comes time for the formal performance appraisal, the starting point is the 'customer' – the affected party – and each individual's performance is measured against these criteria. In schools, for example, teachers can be assessed by a process based on student outcomes, school leaders can be assessed by a process based on teacher performance, and so on. As another example, in a bank, the starting point is the teller–customer interaction and this works its way up. In the prestige car dealership I mentioned above, the starting point would be both the service advisor–customer interaction and service technician–customer interaction, and so on. By starting at this 'grass roots' level a totally different dynamic emerges and relevance is immediately apparent to everyone because the assessment is based on interactions that are seen to occur on a daily basis – and the immediate superior is constantly reminded of his or her responsibility to create and maintain an environment in which their reports can be successful. In other words, the performance appraisal of each person is simultaneously part of the performance appraisal of their boss! Of course, everything still feeds into the same KPIs and KRAs but the overall process for assessing performance is quite different.

Support for this approach of involving a wide range of people was found in a blog in *Harvard Business Review* in December 2012. In a piece entitled 'In a Change Effort, Start with the Last Mile',[7] Ron Ashkenas of Schaffer Consulting in the US pointed out that phenomenal results can be achieved when people who are affected by any change – suppliers, customers, front-line staff and so on – are fully involved in developing the change process. This new approach to performance appraisal ensures such involvement in what the organisation is seeking to achieve and heightens commitment and engagement at every level.

A high-performing organisation will only remain as such if it is comprised of people who are engaged with and committed to their actual tasks, to their peers, and to their organisation. If they cannot see direct relevance between all aspects of performance management and what the organisation is trying to achieve, the probability of maintaining this engagement and commitment is low. My experience is that totally rethinking the performance appraisal system and linking it directly with the impact individual, group and organisational outputs have on the users of those outputs goes a long way to facilitating and maintaining a high-performing organisation.

Chapter Summary

This chapter has explored the issue of the individual in developing and maintaining a high-performing organisation. It has stressed that:

- A high-performing organisation is totally dependent on the people working in the organisation – and the CEO and executive group are only a small part of these.

- High-performing organisations avoid the extremes of either too high or too low a labour turnover.

---

7   http://blogs.hbr.org/ashkenas/2012/12/in-a-change-effort-start-with.html?utm_source=feedburner&utm_medium=feed&utm_campaign=Feed%3A+harvardbusiness+%28H BR.org%29&utm_content=Google+Reader&goback=.gde_63688_member_195048969.

- High-performing organisations understand the capabilities that they currently have and the capabilities that they are going to need. They recruit and develop their people in accord with these capabilities.

- In high-performing organisations the difference between training, education and development is clearly understood and attention is paid to ensuring that all people receive, and are fully supported in, appropriate aspects of human resource development for both their present position and future needs.

- High-performing organisations use a different approach to performance appraisal from that used in ordinary organisations.

- The real measure of whether or not an organisation is 'high performing' is found by understanding the effect that the outputs of individuals and groups (as well as the organisation overall) has on the users of these outputs – in other words the internal and external customers.

The Fifth Step to Obtaining a High-performing Organisation

Consider your own organisation – the one in which you work:

- Thinking back over the way in which cost reduction and/or cost containment measures have been introduced and implemented in the past, does your organisation see its people as an expense or an investment?

- How does your organisation calculate the true cost of labour turnover?

- To what extent does your organisation recruit new employees on the basis of the capabilities the organisation needs now and will need in the near future?

- How could your organisation improve its recruitment and selection process?

• Does your organisation distinguish between the human resource development functions of training, education and development? How could such distinction assist in the evaluation of human resource activities?

• How involved are your managers and supervisors in the human resource development activities of their people? How could a greater level of involvement assist your organisation to become (or continue as) a high-performing organisation?

• What is the real (as opposed to the stated) commitment to performance appraisal in your organisation? How could the performance appraisal process be improved so that it receives the attention and support that it should have?

6

Leading the High-performing Organisation

As the Leadership for Performance model made clear, leadership is the hub around which rotates everything that impacts on the issue of performance. In this chapter we will consider the evolution of leadership thought and practice so that we can understand and apply the leadership that will bring about and maintain a high-performing organisation in this first half of the twenty-first century.

Conventional wisdom has it that the performance of an organisation is almost solely related to its leader. Accordingly, if a sporting team is consistently losing, the coach and/or the captain invariably find themselves replaced. Based on the same approach, there are always plaudits for the coach and captain of a sporting team that is consistently winning.

But what is the truth?

In researching for my book *Leaders: Diamonds or Cubic Zirconia*,[1] I found a common theme from the people I interviewed. This theme argued that there is a distinction between leaders and leadership. The person in charge of an organisation (be it political, religious, social or business) tends to be seen as a leader because he or she heads up that particular organisation. This is unfortunate because, in far too many instances, the person concerned, while emphasising authority and control, often has little – if any – real leadership competence.

The people I interviewed across Australia, New Zealand, Indonesia, Singapore, Malaysia, Thailand, Hong Kong, Taiwan, South Korea and Papua

---

1   Long, Douglas G., *Leaders: Diamonds or Cubic Zirconia – Asia Pacific Leaders on Leadership*, CLS, Sydney, 1998. Reissued in 2012 by Blurb Books, USA.

New Guinea described leadership. In general, they talked of this in terms of having a very specific goal or vision that is communicated in such a way as to get commitment to this vision's realisation and they spoke of the need for a combined effort across the organisation in getting there. When asked for examples of leadership, some of the people interviewed, however, demonstrated a problem. They stated that they had difficulty in nominating leaders as opposed to people who are simply heading-up various areas, organisations or bodies.

When pressed on this issue, it became apparent that many so-called leaders are seen to confuse authority and power with leadership, to rely on personal appeal, a forceful or aggressive manner or 'charisma', or to demonstrate a mindset which implies the end justifies the means in obtaining of results. The net effect is confusion between 'leader' and 'leadership' – and of 'leadership' versus manipulation and control.

So what is the difference between a 'leader' and 'leadership'? From my research, the difference is that a 'leader' carries out particular individual activities or demonstrates particular individual behaviours while 'leadership' is the cumulative effect of the individual activities from all the organisation's leaders.

As I have indicated, one of the problems that arise because of this confusion about leader, leadership, and power and control is that people at the top of organisations are assumed to be leaders whether or not they exhibit leadership capabilities. It is not until the balloon bursts that many so-called leaders are shown to not have leadership competence – the emperor without clothes is eventually told the truth and the populace finally concurs with the obvious. When their businesses are going through a period of growth any confusion between leadership competence and power and control is generally ignored because people equate 'success' with 'leadership'. Unfortunately, of course, as the Global Financial Crisis that started in 2007 also made clear, if you've got enough clout then a lack of leadership competence may still be ignored (and in fact rewarded) even though, as a result of activities over which you have presided, the whole world is in financial chaos.

It was this problem at the top of organisations – be they businesses or governments – that prompted some interesting comments by the well-respected economist Jeffrey Sachs of Columbia University.[2] Sachs can almost be seen to be the counter to Janet Daley (see Chapter 1) because he argues that the US is suffering a moral crisis in which market institutions have effectively taken over the role of government and that their emphasis on financial liberalisation and market forces – that are primarily of benefit to them – has taken precedence over morals and social values. Sachs argues that to all intents and purposes we are now controlled by what is effectively a 'corporatocracy' that has brought about an economy of hype, debt and waste that, although achieving economic growth and high incomes for an elite few, has done so at the cost of extreme income inequality, declining trust among members of the society and the public's devastating loss of confidence in the national government as an instrument of public well-being. He argues that extreme commercialism in which the emphasis is on personal gain (and which, in its current form, originated in and both has been and is actively promoted by the USA's corporate power brokers) has resulted in inequality, corruption, corporate power, environmental threats and psychological destabilisation. The result is that we have a society of markets, laws and elections but he sees these as being nowhere near enough if the rich and powerful fail to behave with respect, honesty and compassion towards the rest of society and towards the world. He argues that the US has developed the world's most competitive market society but that it has thrown away any real sense of social responsibility along the way. Sachs makes a very strong case for economic reform in which many (if not all) of the existing loopholes that allow for those earning excessively high incomes (which some consider as totally out of proportion to the rest of society) are closed and that the most tax is paid by those who earn the most. Sachs wants us to return to a 'mindful' society in which social responsibility receives at least as much attention and emphasis as does personal wealth and economic success.

The on-going impact of the Global Financial Crisis that started in 2007 has put sharply focused attention on this loss of any real sense of social responsibility. In late 2012 events in the European Economic Community because of the problems in such countries as Greece and Spain, and the subsequent demands for fiscal rectitude to precede any form of bailout, has also focused this concept of a 'mindful' society in both the US and in Australia.

However, on March 18, 2003 Australia's ABC TV screened a programme on its 4Corners segment entitled 'The Untouchables'[3] which partly explained

---

2   Sachs, Jeffrey, *The Price of Civilisation: Economics and Ethics after the Fall*, The Bodley Head, Random House, London, 2011.
3   http://www.abc.net.au/4corners/stories/2013/03/18/3715426.htm, March 18, 2013.

why a 'mindful society' is still a long way off. In this programme 4Corners questioned why, following the Global Financial Crisis, no senior people on Wall Street had faced any form of prosecution for criminal behaviour despite the fact that a number of law enforcement officers believed that it would be possible to prove that serious offences had occurred. The programme claimed that officials at the very top of the US Government's Administration (including the US Attorney General) had allowed political considerations to outweigh the pursuit of justice.

The issue of politics dominating any possibility of a mindful society was also illustrated in the so-called Fiscal Cliff that the US faced in December 2012 and again in March 2013. At the end of 2012 the economic focus in the US surrounded legislation that was passed a few years ago which, in return for temporary relief to the USA's financial issues, created a situation where, from January 1, 2013, there would be very significant tax hikes, huge reductions in military spending, and other drastic deflationary measures. In order to avoid what has been termed this 'fiscal cliff', both the US Congress and its Senate were faced with passing urgent economic measures that would allow the country to function effectively from midnight on December 31, 2012. It was claimed that the impact of not reaching agreement between Democrats and Republicans and getting the new measures passed was that the US would face a high probability of falling into at least a major recession and, at worst, a major depression that would, as in the Great Depression of the late 1920s drag the rest of the world with it. The deadline of December 31 passed with temporary agreement given until March 2013 but, during this period, agreement was not reached and, despite the prophecies of doom, as at April 2013, the US economy has not collapsed.

The truth is that, in the US just like anywhere else, almost always vested interests in both business and politics – Democrats and Republicans – focus on their own ideologies and interests rather than on what is really best for both the US and the rest of the world. Many economic commentators are currently saying that unless those running the US are able to take some drastic action, the US economy is a disaster just waiting to happen – they say that the question is 'when' rather than 'if'. There is a belief in some quarters that the era of USA's world dominance is over and that we are witnessing the struggles of a dying empire.

But the US is not alone in this matter of vested interests dominating.

In Australia the situation is more localised. Australia, a country of about 25 million people in a land mass roughly the same size as the continental USA, comprises six States and two Territories. Each of these jurisdictions has an Independent Commission Against Corruption (ICAC) or similar body that is there to investigate possibly corrupt behaviour by politicians and public servants in their dealing with the public and/or in their general stewardship. In Australia's most populated State, New South Wales (NSW) where the major city, Sydney, comprises approximately one-fifth of Australia's total population, the ICAC was formed in 1987 and this body has developed a formidable reputation for ferreting out truth from extremely convoluted and complex dealings. ICAC has wide-ranging powers including various surveillance measures that include telephone taps and accessing phone records, emails, bank accounts, and any other records that may be linked directly or indirectly with the parties under investigation. Failure to cooperate with or to give the truth to ICAC is a serious criminal offence punishable by terms of imprisonment and, from all accounts and appearances, being called to appear before ICAC even as a witness for the prosecution is a harrowing experience. Most of ICAC's hearings are held in public and they are widely reported in all media.

While making it very clear that, as at April 2013, hearings by ICAC about the following issue are still under way and ICAC have made no determination for or against any person or body, late in 2012 ICAC commenced public hearings around the granting of mining licences in the Bylong Valley – an area quite close to Sydney. It is alleged that at least one, and possibly more, men who, at the time the licences were granted, were elected members of the NSW State Government, acted corruptly in that secret and confidential information was shared and, because of access to this knowledge, the family and connections of one, Eddie Obeid, stood to gain some $100 million in a period of only a few months from an initial outlay of around $3.5 million. As at April 2013 the ICAC investigations had interrogated a number of Sydney's rich and powerful people and some would contend evidence provided at these hearings illustrates that, in order to make personal gain, some people will go to almost any length in their attempts to hide possibly illegal, and almost certainly immoral, behaviour. It is alleged by ICAC that vested interests by some politicians and business people including some at the Cabinet level of the State have paid attention primarily to furtherance of their own wealth rather than to the proper stewardship of major State assets. When, later in 2013, their findings are released they will make interesting reading!

While obviously different in scale, these examples are not totally dissimilar from the earlier quoted piece (Chapter 2) by the economist Paul Krugman, who expresses concern about a board seeking to find alternative reasons for awarding their CEO a bonus even though the agreed performance measures were not being met. In Krugman's example it appears that the board were more interested in what was good for the CEO rather than in what was best for the organisation.

The point being made is that those at the top of any organisation – be it politicians or company directors – set the overall moral tone for everyone else. No matter what is said, what these people do will be watched and, as in the case of the USA's approach to the 'fiscal cliff' or the Obeid's purchase of land in the Bylong Valley, others will follow the example set by their 'leaders' and, far too often, self-interest will tend to triumph over the public good right down to the grass roots level. When there is immoral behaviour at the top, don't be surprised to find it also at the bottom!

Directors would do well to study Sachs and Krugman (as well as Sir John Harvey-Jones) and consider their arguments as they pursue the board's role of corporate leadership. While it is certainly true that today many of those heading our major institutions are lacking in real leadership competence and that this has been a major contributor to the world's economic turmoil, it is also true that people with very real leadership competence may not be successful because of circumstances beyond their control. The board needs to create the right environment for long-term success – and that, as Sachs argues, is something many are failing to do. A sporting coach or captain may be working with a team whose members are of mediocre ability, even though very enthusiastic and committed. If this team consistently plays opponents with equal commitment but greater ability then probably they will experience more losses than wins and there is little, if anything, that the coach or captain can do to change the situation other than replacing the players. This course of action, however, may not be a viable option in light of the constraints under which the coach and/or captain have to work – it may even be dysfunctional in light of other factors.

This is equally true in business, politics and so on. While it is true that the person heading such an organisation is generally credited with the success or failure of that organisation, I suggest it is the overall quality of 'leadership' provided in the organisation that ultimately determines whether or not an organisation is successful – and this leadership is found not just in the CEO and executive team. Accordingly it is possible for an organisation to be successful despite the overall organisational head. Equally it is possible for an organisation to be unsuccessful if, despite the leadership, factors other than leadership competence are dominant.

It is this message that the Leadership for Performance model seeks to portray. It talks of leadership and, in so doing, it encompasses the full conceptual aspects of leadership – dealing with individuals and teams, dealing with organisational factors and dealing with the external environment in the quest to ensure desired results. No matter who is the nominal 'leader' of an organisation, the exercise of leadership from at least some additional senior people is critical if performance is to be obtained and maintained in both the short term and long term.

Traditional leadership training has presented the true, yet partial message that no matter where we may be in an organisation, we can still exercise leadership. As stated, this is true yet partial. It is true because leadership is not dependent upon being at the top of an organisational structure. Equally it is partial because if the people at the very top of an organisation are not themselves committed to the principles and practice of effective leadership then we can use our leadership competence, at best, only within the narrow confines available to us and, at worst, not at all. We will be successful only so long as our exercise of leadership practices does not cut across the way in which our superiors expect us to act. The more authoritarian the organisation, the more this limitation is true.

The Leadership Environment

As I mentioned earlier, a major researcher, Elliott Jaques, made the point some years ago that leadership is not a generic concept. He argued that you can only really understand and/or develop leadership when you recognise the context within which leadership is being provided.[4] His point is that effective leadership is always dependent upon a range of factors and the way in which it is exercised can vary significantly across the levels, areas and types of organisations in which people live and work.

---

4   Jaques, Elliott and Clement, Stephen, D., *Executive Leadership: A Practical Guide to Managing Complexity*, Oxford: Blackwell Publishing, 1994.

High-performing organisations consider this carefully and make sure it is recognised and applied. Accordingly they ensure people at different levels are able to fulfil leadership roles appropriate for their position.

BOARD LEADERSHIP

Ultimately it is the board that sets the tone for leadership throughout the organisation. Where a board is functioning as a cohesive body – which does *not* mean that disagreement and discussion are at all stifled – then it operates as an effective operating body that is clear about its governance responsibilities and which fully recognises that, ultimately, the success or failure of the organisation rests upon its collective shoulders. As Jeffrey Sachs argues in the aforementioned book, it is also the case that the board actually sets the moral and ethical tone for the organisation – if an organisation has moral or ethical lapses (and of recent years we've seen myriad examples of these right throughout the world) then it is on the shoulders of the board that the ultimate blame should rest.

One of my roles as a consultant is to assist boards in assessing their effectiveness. I have a series of questionnaires that are answered by each director on a 'peer assessment' basis. From the use of these questionnaires over many years I have developed indicative norms against which the responses can be compared. The full report is provided to the chairman and deputy chairman while each director receives a report which provides them with their personal information but which does not identify any other set of responses. While all the questions are important for the overall picture, a quick picture can be obtained from responses to, in one questionnaire:

- provides valuable input;

- alert and inquisitive;

- meeting preparation;

- long-range planning contribution.

And in another:

- attends meetings well prepared to evaluate and/or add value to agenda items presented to the board and/or committee;

- keeps current on areas and issues on/about which is asked to deliberate and decide;

- based on contributions made at board meetings, gives the impression of being prepared;

- has good conceptual and theoretical ability;

- supports on-going change and development.

In the surveys I have conducted over the years, I have found an increasingly negative range of responses to the questions relating to 'long-range planning contribution' and 'has good conceptual and theoretical ability'.

Sir Adrian Cadbury[5] sets out the main functions of a board as being:

- to define the company's purpose;

- to agree the strategies and plans for achieving that purpose;

- to establish the company's policies;

- to appoint the chief executive;

- to review the performance of the chief executive and the executive team;

- in all this to be the driving force in the company.

Cadbury also nominates the responsibility of the board chairman as being to ensure:

- that the board provides leadership and vision;

- that the board has the right balance of membership;

- that the board sets the aims, strategy and policies of the company;

- that the board monitors the achievement of those aims;

---

5   Cadbury, Sir Adrian, *The Company Chairman*, Director Books, London, UK, 1995.

- that the board reviews the resources of people in the company;

- that the board has the information it needs for it to be effective.

As shown in Chapter 2, ultimately the success or failure of an organisation reflects the leadership provided by the board – and especially the chairman. At this level there needs to be a form of leadership that focuses on the long term yet is fully cognisant of the short term, provides clear parameters within which the executive can operate, and sets in train a process that will engender engagement and commitment throughout the organisation. Sadly, either because of ignorance, micro-management, abdication of responsibility, or, in the worst-case scenarios, moral turpitude, criminal behaviour, ignorance or conflict of interest, far too many boards fail in this.

The other key issue in regards to board leadership is the matter of executive remuneration. In Chapter 2 I made the point that there is some debate as to whether or not providing extremely high remuneration to executives actually results in better organisational performance. Long-term high-performing organisations pay attention to this and ensure that there is a perceived equity of remuneration across all levels and all areas of their operations. They are fully aware of the fact that, after some point, remuneration ceases to be an appropriate reward and instead becomes (or can become) a status symbol. When the status symbols for individuals take precedence over performance of the organisation then an organisation is on the downward slope. It's almost impossible to maintain a high-performing organisation if people at the grass roots feel disenfranchised by having to fight for any remuneration increase while those at the top receive what many believe to be remuneration that is well in excess of any proportion to their actual performance – especially if those 'down the line' have seen their own or other organisations go through some form of decline following a change of CEO or other circumstances beyond their control.

EXECUTIVE LEADERSHIP

If it is the board that is responsible for setting the tone of the leadership throughout an organisation, it is the executive that operationalises and models this leadership. In terms of how the organisation functions on a day-by-day basis, it is the executive who establish (or who fail to establish) an environment in which the organisation can be successful. In Chapter 3 I explained that the executive is responsible for the operational aspects of an organisation. In other words, in terms of obtaining and maintaining a high-performing organisation it is at the executive leadership level 'where the rubber meets the road'.

A tool that I have found very helpful for executives is provided by the Adizes Corporation (Figure 6.1). On their website[6] they offer a free analysis that, based on information input by the executive, makes clear an organisation's current location on its organisational life cycle and highlights both dangers and opportunities. On this life cycle, the optimum location for an established organisation – the area where a high-performing organisation is not only a possibility but also a probability – is 'prime'. While Adizes also offers to assist organisations understand and move on once this analysis is completed (and Adizes should be considered as a very valuable resource for any organisation), in some cases, I have found that simply getting this very valuable and totally unbiased feedback provides an impetus for internally-driven improvement.

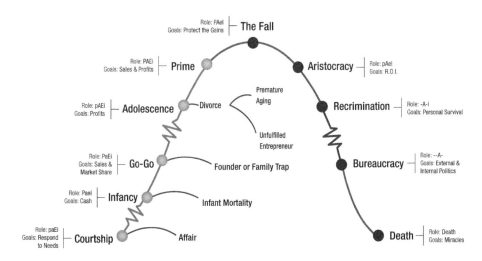

Figure 6.1   Adizes life cycle of an organsation
Source: Reproduced with kind permission from the Adizes Institute.

The power of a tool such as this is that it provides a clear and unambiguous point from which to start on the Vision into Action process. By understanding where the organisation is now executives can look towards their desired position on the life cycle and this leads to the dream with a date, objectives and strategic orientation that will be required to move forward. Without such an analysis as a starting point there is a reasonable probability that any leadership initiatives

---

6   http://adizes.com/of.

could be based on a 'PHOG' approach where 'PHOG' means Preconceptions, Hope, Opinion and Guess – and PHOG is an all too frequent substitute for using accurate data! (I'm not sure of where I got this acronym from but to whoever was the originator, thank you!)

Executive leadership is qualitatively different from managerial leadership. Executive leadership is responsible for developing and achieving the dream with a date through the determining and implementation of objectives and strategies. In other words, executive leadership is focused on the medium to long-term aspects of an organisation – generally a time span of five or more years. Of course the executive needs to be aware of what is going on in the short to medium term (and a failure in this regard can easily mean the downfall of the organisation) but, in high-performing organisations, executives concentrate on enabling their managers to actually deal with the day-by-day aspects of achieving results – they avoid any perception of micro-managing their reports (in fact, if someone is micro-managing, it is clear that he or she is failing in some or all aspects of recruitment, selection, human resource development or overall leadership). This dual vision is especially important in a fast-moving organisation. Let me illustrate.

For one of my recent birthdays, the family gave me a voucher for a rally car driving experience – drive two different cars, each for eight laps, then do a 'hot lap' with an experienced (and in my case, luckily, a very successful) rally car driver. It was great fun. I thoroughly enjoyed it and I learned quite a bit about handling a car under vastly different conditions from what are experienced in day-to-day road driving. The main lesson was to focus on the horizon while being very aware of what was immediately in front of the car. The instructor stressed that the faster the car was going and the more difficult the terrain, the more crucial was the need for a long-range focus combined with very short-range awareness. For me this was a powerful metaphor of the role of an executive in any organisation. Perhaps every executive should be encouraged to do a rally driving experience followed by a discussion as to how they function in the workplace!

This idea of a long-range focus combined with very short-range awareness is quite different from what happens in many organisations. Time and again I find organisations struggling because executives have become so locked in to micro-managing their areas – very short-range awareness – that they are totally unable to do what they are actually supposed to do – demonstrate a long-range focus. Invariably this imbalance results in managers failing to make decisions within an appropriate time frame (or, almost as frequently, passing the decision up the chain) because they find themselves spending exorbitant amounts of time trying to second guess their boss so as to avoid any unpleasant consequences should things not turn out as desired. All too often the end result is either total inertia or the old military 'snafu' (situation normal, all fouled up) of order, counter order, disorder!

Completing the Adizes analysis tool is even more powerful in these situations. The Adizes questionnaire asks a short series of very thought provoking questions about the respondent's perception of their organisation. In my experience, different executives at the same level in the same organisation will often have vastly divergent perceptions that are demonstrated in quite different responses. The result is that, when the various assessments are shared, one could easily think that totally different organisations were being assessed. That is why I always start any intervention with having executives use the tool then bring the results to a 'full and frank' discussion as to where the organisation lies on the life cycle and how it can be moved to (or continue in) 'prime'. And, although I have no connection whatsoever with the Adizes organisation, it's nice to know that, if a person wishes, the Adizes company offers an excellent additional resource that is available on demand.

MANAGERIAL LEADERSHIP

Managerial leadership is the level at which most leadership development interventions focus. The reason for this is that the more senior one is in an organisation, the more it seems to be assumed that leadership will have been learned on the way up. Of course this assumption also appears to presume that the type of leadership provided should remain virtually the same no matter at what level one works. As has already been said, this assumption is now being seriously challenged because it is becoming increasingly apparent that the type of leadership required does change with one's progression through an organisation.

At this managerial level, the leadership required is primarily one-with-one or one-with-small-group and it is focused on the short to medium-term aspects of an organisation – generally a time span relating to the current 12 months.

Traditionally managerial leadership is all about control. In part this is what has led to the much discussed distinction between 'management' and 'leadership' that led at least one writer[7] some years ago to suggest that

---

7   I think it was Professor Warren Bennis who said this when he was at University of Southern California.

'management is about doing things right: leadership is about doing the right thing'. Certainly when I was a young person I was told that 'managers are people who make and implement decisions'. In the past that definition has been fine. Because we lived in a world where it was far easier to control information and where there was a greater propensity to accept authority, managers could exercise power and control partly because of their position in the organisation's hierarchy and partly by the provision or withholding of information. But today we no longer live in that world. Things such as the internet, mobile telephony and social networking have brought about a world in which virtually anything about anyone can be discovered providing a person is prepared to put in the time to search and has the wisdom to distinguish between accurate information and misinformation – both of which are available in large doses.

The matter of good managerial leadership flowing down from good board leadership and good executive leadership is vital in a high-performing organisation. Whereas only a relatively few years ago, staying with an organisation longer than about five years was quite common and most employment was on a full-time basis, today employment on a casual basis is rapidly becoming the norm for a great many people. With this change in employment conditions comes no security of employment and, usually, few if any benefits other than money. Additionally the rise of imports from across the world and the globalisation of almost all national economies mean that organisations want and need their people to be highly productive very quickly after commencing employment. If people are not highly productive very quickly, then, because of the nature of their employment, turning over staff is nowhere as onerous as it once was (although arguably it is more expensive than ever before!). Under such conditions it's a little like the old joke about cleaning out the swamp – when you're up to your arse in alligators, its hard to remember what you are supposed to be doing. If the board and executive have failed or are failing in their leadership responsibility, accountability and effectiveness then don't be surprised if your management's effectiveness is mediocre and/or confused. (Similarly, the corollary applies. If your management's effectiveness is mediocre and/or confused, then take a good hard look at the board and executive because the odds are that the source of the problem is found at the very top.)

Managers are responsible for determining and achieving goals, through application of tactics, and for determining roles and responsibilities within an organisation.

In many ways, managers are 'the meat in the sandwich in organisations' – they are under pressure from the executive to achieve results and they are under pressure from their reports to allow flexibility and innovation in their work. Very often these two pressures are seen to be mutually exclusive – certainly this can be the case under a traditional management concept when controls are rigid, deadlines are tight and costs are under extreme scrutiny. And, if the demands or expectations of a manager's direct reports are not met then, because the concept of organisational loyalty has been destroyed (primarily by the actions of executives focused on cutting costs by dramatically reducing staff and/or increased use of casual rather than full-time staff), the option of staff walking out and leaving the manager in the lurch is an ever-present possibility. Of course, when that happens, even more pressure is exerted downwards on the manager who is still expected to achieve the same results even though he or she has fewer resources available.

Under such circumstances it doesn't take very long before there is a somewhat negative culture in the organisation and everyone gets blamed except those who can (and should) actually do something about it – the board and executive team – because ultimately the responsibility for creating an environment in which everyone can be successful lies on their shoulders. Instead what tends to happen is that managers are 'counselled' and/or sent on various management and/or leadership programmes even though, because of the culture, there is only a low probability of even the very best of these fully achieving the results desired. In turn this brings about the cynicism and 'prisoner of war' mentality in managers that, as everyone involved in human resource development knows, can often permeate the very best training rooms and can have a negative impact on everyone attending the programme.

When everything else is properly in place, it is on the shoulders of managers that the responsibility rests for facilitating the engagement of people with their job, their peers and their organisation. When such engagement really exists then people accept responsibility for their own actions and they see themselves as fully accountable for the quality and quantity of output. When this happens n organisation is well on the way to high performance. But there will not and cannot be a high-performing organisation with highly effective managers unless the board and executive have created the right environment – and that needs both real leadership and also, in many cases, a very different form of leadership from that which currently pertains.

Popular Leadership Approaches

It is only of relatively recent years that leadership has become a serious subject in its own right.[8] Although leadership has been practised and discussed for countless years most of the modern understandings had their genesis in studies that commenced around 1939. Probably the best known of these early studies are those of the late 1940s at Ohio State University which were able to provide a simple (but not simplistic) understanding of two key factors (or 'independent yet related variables') that affect leadership effectiveness. These two factors can be summarised as relating both to people and to the work to be done. A significant number (still possibly the majority) of leadership development approaches provided today can be seen to owe some allegiance to these studies and certainly, at least until the 1990s, this was the dominant base underlying most programmes provided. Alongside this Ohio State Leadership Studies base, at all times, but probably most obvious from the late 1970s however, research indicated alternative approaches and today there is increasing awareness that leadership is one of the most complex issues with which organisations have to grapple – it's a lot more complex than the interaction of two independent yet related variables.

An important aspect of most leadership approaches is the matter of 'leadership style'. Leadership style can be described as 'the pattern of the leader's behaviour as perceived by others'. In other words, although a leader may use a variety of approaches in his or her interaction with others, there will be a set of behaviours with which he or she is most comfortable and it is these behaviours that others will use to describe the leader when asked. Common descriptive terms that may be used include autocratic, authoritarian, democratic, supportive and so on. It was mainly the situational approaches to leadership (see below) that drew attention to this matter of 'leadership style' and in which the ability to adapt one's style became a key concern.

In very broad terms, there seem to be three main approaches to leadership and, while I am discussing only a few of the available approaches, most available leadership development material seems to approximate one of these or to have evolved from them.

---

8   One of the best summaries of leadership research and approaches over the years is found in Bass, Bernard M., *Bass and Stogdill's Handbook of Leadership: Theory, Research, and Managerial Applications*, 3rd edn, The Free Press, New York, 1990.

SITUATIONAL OR CONTINGENCY[9]

Because managerial leadership is primarily one-with-one or one-with-small-group, situational or contingency approaches are very popular ones for providing effective leadership at this level. Situational or contingency approaches to leadership argue that the behaviour of the leader should be dependent upon the situation existing at any time. In the contingency approach the argument is that leaders should be moved around an organisation so that their leadership style is compatible with specific situations encountered while, in situational approaches, the argument is that a leader should be able to modify his or her leadership style in order to suit the situation encountered. Although most situational approaches acknowledge that there are many factors impacting on any situation, as a general rule they see the key situational factor as being the competence and confidence (another two independent yet related variables) of the followers and so it is to the leader–follower interaction that most emphasis is given.

The beauty of these approaches is that, as a rule, they provide a simple diagnostic that can be used quickly and effectively in order to match leadership style and situation. In the situational approaches, because they argue that a leader needs to have versatility of styles, they can also lead to developmental programmes that could enable a leader to be more effective across a range of situations.

There are a significant number of different situational and contingency approaches and the main ones argue that the most effective power base for any leader is 'personal power' – the relationship, trust and respect that a leader develops with other people. However they also make it clear that with these approaches a leader will be far more effective if he or she has available, even if it is not used, a reasonable amount of positional power. Accordingly, in practice, even though situational approaches argue that leadership can be exercised from any position in any organisation, their application very often results in a 'top-down' leadership approach that is heavily dependent upon the leader's place in the hierarchy.

Although they can and do bring about organisational change, my impression is that situational and contingency approaches focus primarily on the activities of individual leaders – in other words they concentrate on 'leaders leading'

---

9   There is an excellent explanation of the contingency and situational approaches in Hersey, Paul, Blanchard, Kenneth and Johnson, Dewey E., *Management of Organizational Behaviour: Utilizing Human Resources*, 10th edn, Pearson Prentice Hall, New York, 2008.

rather than on the broader concept of 'leadership' which relates to the overall process of taking an organisation – not just individuals – to some future place.

THE BIGGER PICTURE

Although much of the leadership material developed in the 1960s and 1970s concentrated on individual leader behaviour, there were always researchers looking at the bigger picture. Amongst the many of those looking at the bigger picture, during the 1970s and 1980s, were John Adair, James McGregor Burns, Kouzes and Posner, and, as already shown in earlier chapters Tero Kauppinen, Bo Gyllenpalm and myself.

Although not as widely known as the more populist approaches to leadership and leader development, during the 1970s, John Adair[10] developed a reputation for his concept of what is known as 'Action Centred Leadership'. From research that was totally separate from the Ohio University Leadership studies, Adair, who was inaugural Professor of Leadership Studies at the University of Surrey in the UK, developed what was essentially a whole of organisation approach. In both its development and in its approach to developing leaders, Action Centred Leadership explored (and explores) the experiences of a wide range of past and current leaders. This approach recognises the interconnection of management and leadership that is required if results are to be achieved. Action Centred Leadership is an integrated approach to managing and leading. Adair argues that while leadership and management have much in common, factors such as administration and resource management are specifically 'management' functions while functions such as inspiring others through the leader's own enthusiasm and commitment are specifically leadership functions. Seeing 'leadership' as the core concept from which 'management' evolved, Adair traced the etymology of leadership to an Anglo-Saxon word meaning the road or path ahead; knowing the next step and then taking others with you on it. He saw the etymology of management as coming from the Latin 'manus', meaning hand, and as being more associated with using a system or machine of some kind. His work argued that to be a more effective leader it was necessary to understand some leadership theory, to be aware of how the three areas of task, group and individual activity interact, and to work on the practical applications of general leadership theory in order to select and train leaders effectively. Action Centred Leadership presents a holistic approach to individual, group and organisational effectiveness.

---

10 Adair, John, *Effective Leadership: A Modern Guide to Developing Leadership Skills*, Gower Publishing, London, 1983.

In 1978 James McGregor Burns introduced the concept of transformational leadership[11] which considered the difference between dealing with individuals, groups and entire organisations. Burns argued that to move forward, many organisations needed to be totally transformed. And he saw this as requiring quite a different approach from the 'transactional' approach of interacting one-with-one or one-with-small-group that tended to dominate in some situational, contingency or other generally used approaches. Other writers also followed up on this concept and works such as John Adams' *Transforming Leadership: From Vision to Eesults*[12] made valuable contributions to this concept.

In 1987, James M. Kouzes and Barry Z. Posner followed up on this transformational approach in their book *The Leadership Challenge: How to Get Extraordinary Things Done in Organizations.*[13] In this book they argued that there were five key practices to be used in leadership that will bring about and maintain high-performing organisations. These are:

1.   Challenging the Process;

2.   Inspiring a Shared Vision;

3.   Enabling Others to Act;

4.   Modelling the Way;

5.   Encouraging the Heart.

Kouzes and Posner argue that, regardless of their position in an organisation, any person can exhibit leadership through implementing these five things. They make it clear that failure to challenge the status quo in organisations is a failure in leadership because it allows inefficient or outdated processes to continue with a consequent loss of productivity and performance. At the same time Kouzes and Posner make it clear that its not enough to see what is wrong with something – its important to have a vision as to how things could be and to communicate that to others in such a way that they, too, become committed to making that vision a reality. Like the situational or contingency approaches

---

11 More recent information about this can be found at Macgregor Burns, James, *Transforming Leadership: A New Pursuit of Happiness*, New York, Atlantic Monthly Press, 2003.
12 Adams, John D. (Ed.), *Transforming Leadership: From Vision to Results*, Miles River Press, Virginia, 1986.
13 Kouzes, James M. and Posner, Barry Z., *The Leadership Challenge: How to Get Extraordinary Things Done in Organizations*, Jossey-Bass Inc. Publishers, San Francisco, 1987.

they recognise that these five practices start with the individual, but an important aspect of Kouzes and Posner's work is that for real organisational transformation the practices need to be developed and implemented right across the organisation rather than simply in the behaviours of individual leaders.

Clearly both the work of James McGregor Burns and the Kouzes and Posner material is supportive of and provides a very useful overlay to the Vision into Action approach that was developed by Tero Kauppinen and Bo Gyllenpalm around the same time. In the Vision into Action approach we stressed that when there is a clash between the left side and the right side of the model, a gap opens up and it is the role of leadership to bridge that gap so that both sides are operating in lock-step (Figure 6.2). In other words, leadership is, at least in part, the filling of the gap between what currently exists and what is desired for both individuals and the organisation. But unless the organisational issues are suitable – in other words the culture is right – a simple concentration by any leader on any individual or group has a relatively low probability of long-term effectiveness. Because, almost invariably, this gap between the 'hard' and 'soft' sides of the model is wider than can be bridged by any one individual it is essential that the greatest possible number of people be developed, enabled and encouraged so that as many as possible of the necessary resources are both available *and are engaged and committed to achieving the desired results.*

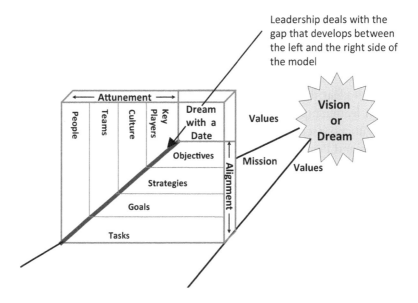

Figure 6.2   Leadership in the Vision into Action model

In 1990 another researcher, Stephen R. Covey[14] suggested that rather than focusing on behaviours, the key to effective leadership was to understand and apply a set of universal principles. He saw this process as starting with the individual but, recognising that leadership was more than just the individual, in Covey's approach, the emphasis then moved so that the universal principles were applied across four organisational levels – personal, interpersonal, managerial and organisational. He saw these key principles as being:

- trustworthiness at the personal level;

- trust at the interpersonal level;

- empowerment at the managerial level;

- alignment at the organisational level.

Covey makes the point that unless there is trust at the personal and interpersonal levels of an organisation a truly high-performing operation is never going to come into existence. This matter of 'trust' or 'credibility' is something that Kouzes and Posner also saw and, having previously implied it, about which they wrote explicitly in 1993[15] and to which I referred in 1998[16] when I raised the issue of 'integrity'. There is a very real sense of futility at the lower levels of an organisation when those leading an organisation, either wittingly or unwittingly, create or allow to develop, an atmosphere of suspicion and mistrust. Unless there is a high level of trust across the organisation then even the best intentions of leaders will bear the stigma of possible manipulation so that 'empowerment' becomes 'second guessing the boss' and encouragement is ignored or ridiculed – and these are immediate (and usually readily apparent to at least an outside observer) signs of an organisation in decline – even if the development of real trust is often ignored by those ultimately responsible for the organisation's performance.

It is for this reason that the issue of organisational culture is so important and why, in the Vision into Action process, it receives so much attention at such an early stage. As I indicated in Chapter 3, from a variety of sources there is strong evidence to suggest that when an organisation's strategic orientation clashes

---

14 Covey, Stephen R., *Principle-Centered Leadership* Fireside, New York, 1990.
15 Kouzes, James M. and Posner, Barry Z., *Credibility: How Leaders Gain and Lose It, Why People Demand It*, Jossey-Bass Inc. Publishers, San Francisco, 1993.
16 Long, Douglas G., *Leaders: Diamonds or Cubic Zirconia – Asia Pacific Leaders on Leadership*, CLS, Sydney, 1998. Reissued in 2012 by Blurb Books, USA.

with its structure then in the long term, culture will dominate. Accordingly an organisation may claim to be 'customer focused' or state that 'we care for our people' but unless the organisational culture supports this all we have are words – and in too many of these cases 'talk is cheap'. This is, in part, why Kouzes and Posner list their fourth leadership practice as 'modelling the way'.

For virtually all organisations, the fact exists that 'what the boss touches is seen to be important' and if the 'boss' seems to think that its perfectly alright to espouse one approach yet model another (and that is inclusive of remuneration!), you can absolutely certain that it is his or her behaviour that will be seen and copied and that the organisation will be nowhere near 'high performing'.

LOMINGER'S LEADERSHIP ARCHITECT

A number of the leadership approaches that have been developed over the years have been criticised on the grounds that some people argue they emphasise intellect and knowledge rather than ability and competence. This concern was addressed by Robert Eichinger and Michael Lombardo who looked at the leadership conundrum in a different way from many others and who developed an approach based on competency rather than intellect. In 1991 they formed Agility Consulting[17] to focus on what are generally known as the Lominger Leadership Competencies. This is a suite of tools that are designed to improve the capability of leaders and organisations. Central to the Lominger approach is a library of competencies that their research indicates are components of effective leadership. Organisations are able to select the competencies that are most appropriate for their leaders at any organisational level, to then assess against these defined competencies, and finally to implement a training programme designed to develop individual competence and organisational capability. This competency-based approach is now widely used across a broad range of organisations.

The Brain's Locus of Control

Recently I suggested a further development in relation to leadership approaches. Over recent years there has been a tremendous growth in new learning from modern neuroscience. Recognising this, and based on research in Australian and British schools, in 2012 I introduced the concept of the brain's

---

17 http://www.lominger.com/about.aspx.

locus of control[18] and the matter of how this impacts on the way we all operate as leaders. In this book I said:

> *Neuroscience has found that one's locus of brain control is complex but basically centred in the combination of several brain areas. Mowat et al. called the reptilian-limbic combination The Red Zone and the neocortical-limbic combination The Blue Zone ... The concept of 'red zone' and 'blue zone' ... refer to our brain's areas (or 'loci') of control.*

I illustrated these zones as shown in Figure 6.3.

I went on to say:

> *When using these terms to describe the brain's loci of control it is important to note that they are simply a shorthand expression relating to a field of study that is very complex and still developing. There is much more to modern neuroscience than is implied in this simple model but, from the perspective of understanding leadership development from*

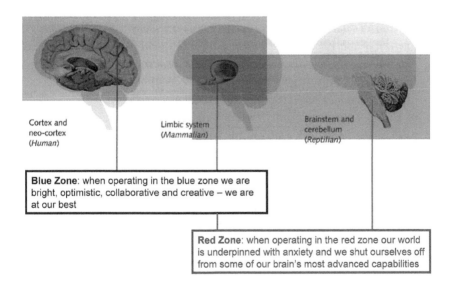

Figure 6.3 **'Red zone–Blue zone'**

---

18 Long, Douglas G. *Third Generation Leadership and the Locus of Control: Knowledge, Change and Neuroscience*, Gower Publishing Limited, Farnham, 2012.

First Generation Leadership to Third Generation Leadership, these are the key areas of interest because they refer to the brain's possible areas for the control of our attitudes and behaviours.

When the brain's area of control is centred in the red zone, the emphasis is on survival. This is the part of the brain that leads to perception of threat (real or imagined) and so to the 'fight, flight, or freeze' syndrome that we see particularly in reptiles and lower level animals. There is no conscious thought in this. Life just 'is' or 'isn't' – it is not something of which the animal is consciously aware – and instinct makes us want to hold on to life if possible so we respond to threat in a way that offers the chance of living another day.

When this perceived threat is physical (for example we are threatened with violence or are in danger of being run over by a bus) then the dominance of the red zone is essential. Instinctive action is required and occurs. Unfortunately, however, because the red zone is dominated by the reptilian brain it is not capable of distinguishing between real threats or imagined threats and so it reacts in the same way whether or not a threat actually exists. In the modern world, a red zone locus of control can lead to some very inappropriate responses when a person perceives a threat even when there is no such intent from other parties and we see this all too frequently in some domestic, social, business, national and international events. Red zone locus of control also leads to the commonly encountered issue of resistance to change.

When the brain's area of control is in the blue zone we have the opportunity to see things differently. Because the blue zone is dominated by the cortical brain – that part of the brain which deals with thought, voluntary movement, language and reasoning (in other words 'with higher level learning') – we have the ability to see things as they actually are and to distinguish between real and imagined threats. This enables us to make a more appropriate response and to find ways of dealing with 'the new' in exciting and innovative ways. When operating with a blue zone locus of control we are better able to deal with complexity and ambiguity than is the case when we operate out of a red zone locus of control.

It must be noted, however, that this 'red zone–blue zone' dichotomy has nothing to do with our emotions. The areas of the brain that brings about emotion are common to both the blue zone and the red zone. In other words, it is not a case of 'red zone = unhappy' 'blue zone = happy' or anything like that. People with their brain's locus of control in the blue zone will have exactly the same range of emotions as they have always had. Any difference will relate to the way in which these emotions are handled.

What modern neuroscience has done is to enable us to add another layer to the leadership process. By understanding how the brain's area of control impacts on our everyday behaviour and by learning how to manage down the red zone while simultaneously managing up the blue zone we are able to take a new look at the whole concept of leadership and to discover totally new ways of dealing with the issues that we are facing today as well as those that will emerge in coming years.

In the first decade of the twenty-first century, we have encountered a situation in which the working hours of western industrialised countries seem to be increasing. There seems to be an assumption that employees, particularly in 'white collar' jobs, should be prepared to work whatever hours are required to meet targets set by their bosses. Very often it seems that those in management and executive positions are expected to be available 168 hours a week (or '24/7') and to have no interests or involvements other than their work. In many ways we seem to have regressed to the situation that pertained over 100 years ago.

From reading newspapers as well as from talking with people, the impression is gained that many people today are scared of taking leave that is due or even of seeking medical and/or dental treatment that might be required because time away from the workplace could be penalised in the next round of layoffs or cost-cutting. We encounter situations in which companies crash, with employees, minor creditors and small stockholders left out of pocket – sometimes while directors, executives, the banks and other major creditors continue to receive their monies due or deemed due because of 'performance' clauses in contracts. In the event of non-executive employees seeking to protect their interests we are still likely to encounter similar anti-union views to those which permeated society in the earlier years of the twentieth century – the workers and their supporters are vilified for daring to want security of entitlements.

The French have a proverb which goes something like 'plus ça change, plus ça reste la meme chose' – the more things change, the more they stay the same. We need a new approach – something that is a real change in the way we do things.

While our physical evolution has seen tremendous changes in our physical attributes (for example, today we tend to be taller and heavier than was the case a few thousand years ago) our neurological evolution hasn't moved quite as fast. Our ancient ancestors needed to have a dominant 'red zone' because of the very nature of survival in the days of a hunting and gathering society. Today our society is vastly different yet we have maintained societal norms of power and control that maintain our red zone dominance – this is why creating a sense of fear is such a powerful tool. Creating a sense of fear and/or indignation at the behaviour of others is frequently used by unscrupulous politicians and managers in order to gain ends that suit their personal agendas regardless of what is really best for society and/or the organisation. Many of the current attitudes and actions relating to the treatment of refugees by a wide range of countries is a case in point. It is because our organisational leaders, like the rest of society (including – and perhaps especially – our political leaders), are locked into the red zone as their default position that we continue to have the sort of 'them and us' confrontations. An example of this 'them and us' issue in industrial relations is reflected in recent comments made by the Australian Industry Group (AIG)[19] as in a statement towards the end of 2012 it blames unions and workers for inflexibility and argues that unions are primarily to blame for Australian businesses taking their operations off shore – a premise that, as the case study makes clear, would be debated by Briysun.

And herein lies the core of the problem in applying traditional leadership approaches and development no matter what they might be. It's a lot easier to find a scapegoat than it is to look in the mirror and accept that I am less than perfect!

If our default mindset is one of suspicion and apprehension – one in which we are worried that we might be exploited or that someone else might get an unfair advantage over us, then we will, subconsciously at least, seek to preserve what we feel is or should be 'ours'. This is 'red zone' attitude and behaviour in which vague, possible fears, bring us to the instinctive defensive reactions of fight, flight or freeze – and in none of these is creativity and innovation truly possible. Hence productivity declines and production of desired results

19 http://www.abc.net.au/news/2012-11-16/ai-group-chief-attacks-workplace-laws/4376212, November 2012.

becomes increasingly difficult. The easy way out is then to find a scapegoat – government, international issues, the economy, trade unions, greedy employees, poor management, lazy employees, greedy banks, monetary exchange rates and so on – any scapegoat will do so that we can avoid blaming ourselves and we can justify our failure to look for creative solutions.

What we know from both research and experience is that most people are only able to give their very best when they feel

- emotionally safe;

- unconditionally respected;

- believed in as individuals;

- listened to;

and, in theory at least, these are the conditions that should be brought about by leaders as they seek to achieve performance goals with individuals and organisations.

But, by definition, people operating in the red zone cannot feel emotionally safe because a hallmark of the red zone is, at the best, vague apprehension and, at the worst, debilitating fear. It doesn't matter what a leader may say, unless the leader's behaviour shows that the words are backed up by supportive actions, any attempt by a leader to encourage creativity through honest, upwards feedback and/or criticism has the proverbial snowball in hell's chance of success!

But even if a leader is backing up his or her words with the appropriate behaviour, then it is essential that this appropriate behaviour is consistent *even when it doesn't get the desired response from followers in the short to medium term*. Those who make their money from promoting gambling know that intermittent wins such as are experienced from poker machines, casino games, racing and so on are important because, no matter how much a punter may lose, an intermittent win will fire up the hopes of a big win with the next bet. (Addiction to this hope of the next bet being a big winner is of course one of the main features of problem gamblers – people addicted to gambling.) A similar situation pertains in leadership. No matter how much a follower might want to believe that his or her leader is genuinely looking for suggestions and even criticism, unless the leader consistently exhibits the right behaviour over a protracted period then any slip runs the risk of reinforcing in the follower a belief that the leader is manipulating people and doesn't really mean what is said – unless you are consistently showing the right behaviour, some of your people will always have an underlying suspicion that one day 'the axe will fall'! In other words, unless you, the leader, are operating from the blue zone you should not expect your people or your organisation overall to be a high-performing organisation.

The very good news is that it is possible for everyone to shift their brain's locus of control from the red zone to the blue zone – this is because the shift is behaviourally based and behaviours can be learned.

THIRD GENERATION LEADERSHIP

One of the reasons why situational or contingency approaches tend to be more effective when the leader has positional power is because our dominant paradigm for leadership and management is that the leader must be in control or at least to be thought to be in control. Populist literature and the media tell us that we want and need 'strong' leadership where the leader makes it clear what has to be achieved and in which he or she drives through his or her agenda in order to achieve these results. In the populist view we equate leadership with power, authority and control.

In *Third Generation Leadership and the Locus of Control* I wrote:

> *Third Generation Leadership moves us away from a world based on power and authority: away from a world in which hierarchy is accepted as normal and necessary. Third Generation Leadership moves us away from a world in which the leader knows best. Third Generation Leadership moves us away from a world of compliance, compulsion and/ or conformance. It moves us to a world in which people engage with each other regardless of who they are or where they may be and in which they then engage together in order to achieve whatever performance is desired.*

The characteristics of Third Generation Leadership and 3G Leaders[20] are:

---

20 In *The Success Zone*, Mowat et al. provide detailed information on how to develop these skills. There are also some very valuable examples and tools that can help in the development of both Authentic Leadership and Third Generation Leadership, available in George, Bill and Sims, Peter, *True North: Discover your Authentic Leadership*, Jossey-Bass, San Francisco, 2007.

- *they engage with others as individuals rather than seeking to obtain obedience or compliance;*
- *they are collaborative and facilitative;*
- *they encourage growth and self-directed learning by everyone;*
- *they respect other people even if they are not receiving respect in return;*
- *they invite questions and genuine discussion;*
- *they ask questions with a view to helping others find their own solutions;*
- *they listen to help others engage with their own or shared solutions;*
- *they are totally non-discriminatory in thought, word and action.*

Because of these characteristics, 3G Leaders are able to create environments in which people feel:

- *emotionally safe;*
- *unconditionally respected;*
- *believed in as individuals;*
- *listened to.*

These are the critical conditions for people to be engaged not only with what they do but also with their fellow toilers. And the really good news is that, because these conditions are created by the leader's behaviour they are not some idealistic way of thinking. They are behaviours, and behaviours can be learned.

These leader behaviours create the optimal conditions for organisational and personal success in the twenty-first century – the conditions for achieving desired performance. But to get them, we have to move beyond the existing approaches.

I think it was the Chinese philosopher Lao Tsu who, a great many years ago, said something like:

> *The bad leader is he who the people fear,*
> *The good leader is he who the people revere,*
> *The great leader is he of whom the people say:*
> *'we did it ourselves'.*

Because our default approach is to have our locus of control in the red zone, we tend to be 'cursed' with 'bad' leaders or 'blessed' with 'good' leaders. In either of these cases charisma becomes an essential ingredient – at least for those leaders who concentrate more on form than on substance. But, as Lao Tsu makes clear, in our dominant leadership models both good and bad leadership are based on power, authority and control – the leader is feared or praised for his or her use of power and authority.

High-performing organisations with high levels of productivity are those with 'great' leaders – in other words they are 'Third Generation Leaders' with their brain's locus of control firmly in the blue zone. It is only when we operate from the blue zone that we have sufficient confidence and creativity to fully create an environment in which people can say, 'We did it ourselves'.

It can be argued that, in some respects, it doesn't particularly matter what traditional leadership philosophy or approach you use. The important thing is the mental model that lies behind your leadership activity. And your mental model comes out of your brain's locus of control. Only when leaders operate from the blue zone does it become possible to achieve the levels of engagement and commitment that are essential for high performance – and operating from the blue zone will enable you to implement your preferred leadership approach far more effectively than has ever previously been possible.

As I said in *Third Generation Leadership and the Locus of Control*, in a high-performing organisation – one which is blue zone dominated, the emphasis is on the implementation of leadership that will:

- *Make it very clear that individual accountability is to be the norm and that this accountability is to oneself, one's peers, one's leaders and one's organisation in order to ensure desired results are attained.*
- *Have a very clear set of organisation values that illustrate the importance of seeing and understanding the interacting variables that form any and all organisations. (These values need to be expressed in behavioural terms.)*
- *Ensure there is no disconnect between espoused values and practiced values at senior levels – widespread cognitive dissonance will quickly destroy the veneer that seeks to cover any disconnect.*

- *Use this value set to provide guidelines for everyone on how to deal with the ambiguity and complexity with which every organisation and every individual is faced on an increasingly frequent basis.*
- *Structure the organisation so that leaders at every level obviously and willingly provide a significant 'value-added' component to that which is done by their followers.*
- *Remove any grossly excessive status symbols that are dependent upon one's position in the hierarchy and which make it clear who are 'us' as opposed to those who are 'them'.*
- *Develop a 'no blame' culture in which mistakes are used to facilitate learning and growth instead of being a reason for punishment – if people believe they will suffer penalties for making wrong decisions then they will avoid making decisions.*
- *Develop a cognitive coaching culture in which everyone is encouraged to shift and to maintain their brain's locus of control in the blue zone.*
- *Be very clear about organisational goals and the role each person has in achieving these goals.*
- *Demonstrate trust by ensuring every person in the organisation knows what the organisation is seeking to achieve and, in broad terms, how the organisation intends to achieve these. Be honest and to everyone 'tell the truth, the whole truth, and nothing but the truth'.*
- *Ensure everyone clearly understands what are 'givens' (that is, those things that are not open to debate or question) and those things about which there is flexibility.*
- *For those things for which there can be flexibility, provide very clear parameters within which each person is authorised to make decisions and empower and encourage them to make these decisions.*
- *Encourage open discussion, questioning and contributions relating to what the organisation is doing and how things could be done better. As most consultants know, the people closest to any issue or problems invariably know how the issue could be fixed – their frustration is that, other than the consultant, most people won't listen to them or take their suggestions seriously.*
- *Encourage people to develop interdepartmental networks and to interact informally to resolve issues and to explore possible solutions to the problems and issues being faced.*

Only a Third Generation Leadership approach can bring this about because, again as I said in *Third Generation Leadership and the Locus of Control*:

> *Third Generation Leadership is based on engagement. And engagement requires that people do things – that they follow the leader – because they want to rather than because they have to. Engagement requires that the leader has developed high levels of trust and respect with the followers. When this is done properly the followers become committed to the same course of action as the leader.*

And when this happens you are well on the way to obtaining and maintaining a high-performing organisation.

BECOMING A HIGH-PERFORMING ORGANISATION THROUGH THIRD GENERATION LEADERSHIP

In Chapter 3 I made the point that the keys to effective cognitive coaching are questioning and listening. These two behaviours are also the keys to becoming a Third Generation Leader and to implementing Third Generation Leadership.

There are two questions to ask if you want your organisation to become a high-performing organisation that is based on Third Generation Leadership:

- Is your current leadership approach getting you the results that you want right now?

- Are you reasonably confident that, by maintaining this approach, you will continue to get the results you want in the future?

If the response to both questions is 'yes' then, no matter the reality in relation to any need for development, probably you will not be seriously interested in any change. If the answer to either question is 'no' then possibly you *may* be interested in making some changes – but equally you may not yet have reached the point where you are psychologically ready to make changes. If the answer to both questions is 'no' then you are probably looking for answers and, if that is the case, there is a reasonably high probability that you will consider making the necessary behavioural changes.

The characteristics of Third Generation Leaders are:

- they engage with others as individuals rather than seeking to obtain obedience or compliance;

- they are collaborative and facilitative;

- they encourage growth and self-directed learning by everyone;

- they respect other people even if they are not receiving respect in return;

- they invite questions and genuine discussion;

- they ask questions with a view to helping others find their own solutions;

- they listen to help others engage with their own or shared solutions;

- they are totally non-discriminatory in thought, word and action.

Because of these characteristics, Third Generation Leaders are able to create environments in which people feel:

- personally accountable;

- emotionally safe;

- unconditionally respected;

- believed in as individuals;

- listened to.

These are the critical conditions for people to be engaged not only with what they do but also with their fellow group or team members. And the really good news is that, because these conditions are created by the leader's behaviour they are not some idealistic way of thinking. They are behaviours and behaviours can be learned – even the behaviours of powerful questioning, observational listening and optimistic listening.

These leader behaviours create the optimal conditions for organisational and personal success in the twenty-first century – the conditions for achieving a high-performing organisation.

Chapter Summary

This chapter has explored the issue of leadership in developing and maintaining a high-performing organisation. It has stressed that:

- Leadership is not a generic concept – the exercise of leadership differs both qualitatively and quantitatively depending on a leader's place in the organisational hierarchy and his or her responsibilities.

- High-performing organisations understand and practice leadership that is appropriate for the various levels at which it is being exercised so that, right through the organisation, there is both alignment with the vision and attunement of the various elements that will determine whether or not the dream with a date is attained.

- Popular leadership approaches tend to be either situational/ contingency or whole of organisation and, in both cases, they are generally predicated on the leader having some form of power, authority and control.

- Modern neuroscience has enabled us to add a new dimension to the concept of leadership through understanding the brain's locus of control – either the red zone of fear or the blue zone of courage.

- In high-performing organisations, leaders have their brain's locus of control firmly in the blue zone and this enables them both to create the environment in which high productivity is engendered through creativity and innovation, and also to implement their preferred leadership approach in the most effective manner.

Taking the Next Step with a High-performing Organisation

Consider your own organisation – the one in which you work:

- To what extent is there a clear delineation of leadership approaches and responsibilities throughout the organisation? What can be done to improve this?

- What is the primary leadership development approach used in your organisation? How effectively is it implemented on a day-by-day basis? How could the return on investment from this initiative be improved?

- To what extent do people throughout your organisation feel emotionally safe, unconditionally respected, believed in as individuals and listened to? What could be done to bring about such a culture?

- What do you think could be the benefits to your organisation if people did feel emotionally safe, unconditionally respected, believed in as individuals and listened to?

- What can you personally do to help facilitate an environment in which every person accepts the accountability that is necessary to maintain a high-performing organisation?

- What is your action plan for implementing the processes explained in this book? What first step to implement this action plan are you going to take now?

Additional Resources

For people who would like more in-depth understanding of the concepts introduced and used in this book, the following resources may be of value:

Websites and Articles

http://adizes.com

http://astonjournals.com/manuscripts/Vol2011/BEJ-31_Vol2011.pdf

http://en.wikipedia.org/wiki/DISC_assessment

http://www.myersbriggs.org/my-mbti-personality-type/mbti-basics/

http://www.iza.org/conference_files/Leadership_2012/stanton_c7876.pdf

http://www.lominger.com/about.aspx

http://www.mckinseyquarterly.com/Retail_Consumer_Goods/Strategy_
   Analysis/Encouraging_your_people_to_take_the_long_view_3014,
   September 2012

http://www.mckinseyquarterly.com/Organization/Change_Management/
   Leadership_and_the_art_of_plate_spinning_3037

http://www.mckinsey.com/features/leading_in_the_21st_century/michael_
   useem

http://www.garyhamel.com/ and http://strategos.com/

http://www.mckinseyquarterly.com/Retail_Consumer_Goods/Strategy_
   Analysis/Encouraging_your_people_to_take_the_long_view_3014,
   September 2012

http://www.parliament.wa.gov.au/intranet/libpages.nsf/WebFiles/Hot+
   Topics+-+Shields+report+Executive+salaries/$FILE/Buck+stops+here.pdf

http://www.strategy-business.com/article/19868?gko=04205&cid=20130115ene
   ws&utm_campaign=20130115enews

http://www.telegraph.co.uk/news/politics/georgeosborne/9730434/The-West-
   is-signing-its-own-death-sentence.html

http://blogs.hbr.org/ashkenas/2012/12/in-a-change-effort-start-with.html?
utm_source=feedburner&utm_medium=feed&utm_campaign=Feed%3A+h
arvardbusiness+%28HBR.org%29&utm_content=Google+Reader&goback=.
gde_63688_member_195048969

Books and Other Publications

Adair, John, *Effective Leadership: A Modern Guide to Developing Leadership Skills*, Gower Publishing, London, 1983.

Adams, John D. (Ed.), *Transforming Leadership: From Vision to Results*, Miles River Press, Virginia, 1986.

Bass, Bernard M., *Bass and Stogdill's Handbook of Leadership: Theory, Research, and Managerial Applications*, 3rd edn, The Free Press, New York, 1990.

Beer, Michael and Nohria, Nitin, 'Cracking the Code of Change', *Harvard Business Review*, May–June 2000, p. 133.

Bremer, Marcella, *Organizational Culture Change: Unleashing Your Organization's Potential*, Amazon, USA, 2012.

Burns, James Macgregor, *Transforming Leadership: A New Pursuit of Happiness*, New York: Atlantic Monthly Press, 2003.

Cadbury, Sir Adrian, *The Company Chairman*, Director Books, UK, 1995.

Corrigan, John, *A World Fit for Children*, Castleflag Pty Ltd, Sydney, 2005.

Covey, Stephen R., *Principle-Centered Leadership*, Fireside, New York, 1990.

Deming, W. Edwards, *Out of the Crisis*, Cambridge University Press, Cambridge, 1986.

Doidge, Norman, *The Brain that Changes Itself*, Scribe Publications, 2010.

George, Bill and Sims, Peter, *True North: Discover your Authentic Leadership*, Jossey-Bass, San Francisco, 2007.

Hersey, Paul, Blanchard, Kenneth and Johnson, Dewey E., *Management of Organizational Behaviour: Utilizing Human Resources*, 10th edn, Pearson Prentice Hall, New York, 2008.

Jaques, Elliott, *Time Span Handbook*, Heinneman, London, 1964.

Jaques, Elliott, *Requisite Organization: A Total System for Effective Managerial Organization and Managerial Leadership for the 21st Century*, 2nd edn, Cason Hall and Co, Arlington, VA, 1991.

Jaques, Elliott and Clement, Stephen D., *Executive Leadership, A Practical Guide to Managing*, Basil Blackwell, Inc., Cambridge, MA, 1991.

Kable, Jim, *People, Preferences, and Performance*, John Wiley and Sons, Brisbane, Australia, 1988.

Katzenbach, Jon R. and Smith, Douglas K., *The Wisdom Of Teams: Creating the High Performance Organisation*, Harvard Business School Press, Boston, MA, 1993.

Kolb, David A., Rubin, Irwin M. and McIntyre, James M., *Organisational Psychology*, 4th edn, Prentice Hall, New Jersey, 1984. This is also reflected in the later books by Kolb, Rubin and Osland from 1991.

Kotter, John P. and Heskett, James L., *Corporate Culture and Performance*, The Free Press, New York, 1992.

Kouzes, James M. and Posner, Barry Z., *The Leadership Challenge: How to Get Extraordinary Things Done in Organizations*, Jossey-Bass Inc. Publishers, San Francisco, CA, 1987.

Kouzes, James M. and Posner, Barry Z., *Credibility: How Leaders Gain and Lose it, Why People Demand It*, Jossey-Bass Inc. Publishers, San Francisco, CA, 1993.

Krugman, Paul, *The Conscience of a Liberal*, W.W. Norton, New York, 2009.

Lehrer, Jonah, *The Decisive Moment*, Canongate Books Ltd., Edinburgh, 2009.

Lewin, K. 'Defining the Field at a Given Time', *Psychological Review*, Vol. 50, 292–310. Republished in *Resolving Social Conflicts and Field Theory in Social Science*, Washington, DC, American Psychological Association, 1997.

Long, Douglas G., *Competitive Advantage in the Twenty First Century: From Vision into Action*, CLS, Sydney, 1993.

Long, Douglas G., *Third Generation Leadership and the Locus of Control: Knowledge, Change and Neuroscience*, Gower Publishing Limited, Farnham, 2012.

Long, Douglas G., *Leaders: Diamonds or Cubic Zirconia – Asia Pacific Leaders on Leadership*, CLS, Sydney, 1998. Reissued in 2012 by Blurb Books, USA.

Long, Douglas G., *The Curse of PPM and How to Remove It*, Blurb Books, USA, 2012.

McGregor, Douglas, 'An Uneasy Look at Performance', *Harvard Business Review*, May–June, 1957.

Mintzberg, Henry, 'Patterns in Strategy Formation', *Management Science*, Vol. 24, No. 9, 1978.

Mowat, Andrew, Corrigan, John and Long, Douglas G., *The Success Zone*, Global Publishing, Melbourne, 2010.

Moyes, Allan G., *For Sale: Quality Leadership*, CLS, Sydney, 1997.

Nadler, Leonard, *Corporate Human Resources Development: A Management Tool*, Van Nostrand Company, New York, 1980.

Price, Colin and Keller, Scott, *Beyond Performance: How Great Organizations Build Ultimate Competitive Advantage*, John Wiley and Sons, New Jersey, 2011.

Sachs, Jeffrey, *The Price of Civilisation: Economics and Ethics after the Fall*, The Bodley Head, Random House, London, 2011.

Schein, Edgar H., 'How Can Organisations Learn Faster? The Challenge of Entering the Green Room', *Sloan Management Review*, Winter, 1993.

Senge, Peter, *The Fifth Discipline*, Random Sentry, Inc., New York, 1992.

Stephenson, C., 'What Causes Top Management Teams to Make Poor Strategic Decisions?', 2012, unpublished thesis for the degree of DBA from Southern Cross University, NSW, Australia.

Tuckman, Bruce W. and Jensen, Mary Ann C., 'Stages of Small Group Development Revisited', *Group and Organizational Studies*, Vol. 2, 419–427, 1977.

Yukl, Gary A., *Leadership in Organizations*, 8th edn, Prentice-Hall, New Jersey, 2012.

Index